The Economic System in an Age of Discontinuity

Long-Range Planning or Market Reliance?

THE CHARLES C. MOSKOWITZ MEMORIAL LECTURES

NUMBER XVII

Wassily Leontief

PROFESSOR OF ECONOMICS
NEW YORK UNIVERSITY

Herbert Stein

A. WILLIS ROBERTSON PROFESSOR OF ECONOMICS
UNIVERSITY OF VIRGINIA

The Economic System in an Age of Discontinuity

Long-Range Planning or Market Reliance?

THE CHARLES C. MOSKOWITZ MEMORIAL LECTURES
COLLEGE OF BUSINESS AND PUBLIC ADMINISTRATION
NEW YORK UNIVERSITY

NEW YORK   *New York University Press*   1976

Copyright © 1976 by New York University
Library of Congress Catalog Card Number: 76-15856

ISBN: 0-8147-48970-4

Library of Congress Cataloging in Publication Data

Leontief, Wassily W   1906–
      The economic system in an age of discontinuity.

      (The Charles C. Moskowitz memorial lectures ; no. 17)
      1.   United States—Economic policy—1971–
—Addresses, essays, lectures.   I.   Stein, Herbert,
joint author.   II.   Title.   III.   Series.   IV.   Title:
Long-range planning or market reliance.
HC106.7.L46   330.9'73'0925   76-15856
ISBN 0—8147—4970—4

Manufactured in the United States of America

FOREWORD

The Charles C. Moskowitz Memorial Lectures were established at the College of Business and Public Administration with the purpose of advancing public understanding of issues of major concern to business and to the nation. The donor was the late Charles C. Moskowitz, a remarkably warm, generous, and compassionate human being who was also a distinguished alumnus of the College. He was a pioneer in the American motion picture industry and was one of those who helped develop the film industry from a small beginning to its present position. Through the lecture series the College has been able to magnify its educational scope and to make a significant contribution to public discussion and understanding of important issues affecting the American economy and its business enterprises.

The present volume is the seventeenth in the Charles C. Moskowitz Memorial Lecture Series. All

7

of the lectures have been on topics of great substance and have stimulated lively interest. And most have managed to be in the vanguard of events. They have elucidated major issues which were as yet not clear. The lectures published in this book are in that group, being concerned with the subject of national economic planning in the United States.

The subject of national economic planning has engendered considerable discussion, as well as organized action both inside and outside the Congress of the United States. In the latter connection, Professor Wassily Leontief, one of the Moskowitz lecturers joined Leonard Woodcock, President of the United Auto Workers, in heading the Initiative Committee for National Economic Planning. And Senators Jacob Javits and Hubert Humphrey reflected the Committee's view that economic planning is needed in this nation by placing the proposed Balanced Growth and Economic Planning Act of 1975 before the Senate. It must be noted that those favoring planning include businessmen and political leaders of both major parties, as well as scholars. In short, the roster of names associated with the current proposal does not look like the membership list of some small and peripheral clandestine group. They are people of experience and sophistication who are deeply concerned that today's problems of inflation and unemployment are not and will not be responsive to the fiscal and monetary tools that we have been relying on since World War II.

But many others, of equal experience and

sophistication, are convinced that the prescription—if followed—may prove fatal to the patient. Professor Herbert Stein, also one of our Moskowitz lecturers, has emerged as a major spokesman among that group, which also includes leading businessmen and political leaders. This group is deeply disturbed by the record of government intervention in and regulation of our economy to date, for they find little or nothing in that record to inspire confidence in the idea that government planning and action will improve matters. And they are no doubt deeply worried that further enlargement of government's role will finally and fatally undermine such survival strength as still remains in our private sector and in the market system.

The issue is of profound importance to the future of our nation, and perhaps of the world. It is fortunate that the Moskowitz Memorial lectures provided a forum for bringing together Professors Leontief and Stein to discuss it. It is fortunate too that Israel Kirzner, Professor of Economics at New York University, and Mr. John R. Stark, Executive Director of the Joint Economic Committee of the United States Congress, were able to participate as discussants.

Wassily Leontief, who was awarded the Nobel Prize in 1973 for his pioneering work in input-output analysis and who is now Professor of Economics at New York University, spoke on "National Economic Planning—Methods and Problems." According to Professor Leontief, American society is now suffering serious consequences because of the inability of its badly regulated competitive market mechanism

to satisfy even the minimal requirements of an orderly economy. As a corrective, he suggested
national economic planning. The first step in
preparing a national economic plan, according to
Leontief, would be to develop a statistical matrix
which would describe the economy and its interrelationships. But this matrix also would be
designed to project the state of the economy five and
more years into the future. Most importantly, Leontief calls for alternative plans (or scenarios) which
would be feasible and which would offer us a choice.
Public discussion and democratic choice among concrete tangible alternatives would then follow, with
the final version of the plan being the end product of
"typically American political logrolling and
legislative wrangles." However, the technical planning agency would have the important role, in addition to that of developing feasible alternative
scenarios, of maintaining the overall integrity of the
plan which finally emerged; that is, that the plan does
not call for the allocation of more than can be
produced or, alternatively, that nothing is left over
(for example, no one is left unemployed). It is important to note that Professor Leontief does not en-
visage the death and disappearance of either the
market mechanism or the profit motive. Instead he
sees a planned economy in which "the price
mechanism will be an effective but humble servant of
the society not, as it often is, an overbearing and all
too often fumbling master."

Herbert Stein, A. Willis Robertson Professor of
Economics at the University of Virginia and former
chairman and member of the Council of Economic

Advisers under Presidents Nixon and Ford, spoke on
"Planning the American Economy." Stein began by
distinguishing between unhappiness over the performance of an economy and the adequacy of that
economy. The distinction is significant because it
enables him to observe that people may be unhappy
even though their economy is adequate—or even
more than adequate—because their expectations are
unrealistic and beyond the capabilities of the
economy. Thus, many Americans can be unhappy
over the performance of their market system without
their unhappiness necessarily damning the system.
Turning to planning, he asks rhetorically about its
meaning and proceeds immediately to set forth eight
versions. These range from very moderate plans,
with which he has no quarrel, to strict forms of direction and control, with which he has a profound
quarrel. He identifies "indicative planning" (the
sixth version) as the one which he perceives as being
called for by Leontief and those in agreement with
Leontif. This type of planning is not to be coercive,
but merely to indicate the economy's direction. Stein
attacks this view, arguing that it is unnecessary
because the market mechanism is still the most effective instrument for achieving the basic economic
decisions of resource allocation and income
distribution (with allowance for a much more
moderate degree of government influence than is
presently the case). Perhaps more importantly, he
worries about the vagueness of goals and
mechanisms in the proposals of the "planners." And
he worries too about the danger that freedom will be
supplanted by government dictation, despite the

good intentions of the "planners." Stein hopes that
more and better economic information, more and
better public understanding, and less and easier
regulation of the economy will enable the inherent
power of the market mechanism to reassert itself,
and thereby to overcome the dangers inherent in
national economic planning.

Professor Kirzner's comments are exceptionally
incisive, for he contrasts the "planners" call for
feasible alternative economic scenarios with the
market mechanism's tendency toward optimality.
And he sees the distinction between feasibility and
optimality as critical, for the latter is associated with
personal freedom of choice in ever searching out that
arrangement which is most satisfying or most effective in eliminating gaps in economic coordination. He is plain in his preference for the market
mechanism as he asks: "May it not just be possible
that what our sluggish and fitful patient needs for
recovery is not a heart-transplant, nor even a crash
program of economic research and expanded
gathering of statistics—but simply fresh air, sunshine, good food and exercise, free of the addictive
drug of monetary inflation, of the crushing weight of
a bloated public sector, and of the mass of
regulations which hamper the flow of the spontaneous and invigorating juices of free competition?"

John R. Stark sees the fear of a bloated public
sector as something of a "straw man." To him the
basic test of the strength of the private sector resides
in the fact that almost all income producing assets
are, according to him, privately owned in the United
States. But the Federal Government is powerful

because it sets limitations on the use of property, it transfers income, it regulates, it directs resource allocation—and it does so on a massive scale. Interestingly, Stark is profoundly concerned because he perceives the massive involvement of the Federal Government in the economy to be unplanned, and hence dangerous. The danger arises, in his view, out of the opportunity afforded, as a result of a lack of good government coordination and direction, to power blocs to assert themselves in ways detrimental to general well-being. It is his hope that planning will work, for he considers it to be necessary for the achievement of both a better and a freer life.

I would be remiss if I closed without some words of appreciation for the excellent handling of all aspects of the lectures, as well as for the editorial preparation of this volume. These words are directed to Mrs. Susan Greenbaum, my administrative assistant, and I am most appreciative of her role in guaranteeing the success of the lectures. I appreciate too the work of the staff of the New York University Press in publishing the lectures expeditiously.

Abraham L. Gitlow
Dean
College of Business and
Public Administration

March, 1976

THE CHARLES C. MOSKOWITZ MEMORIAL LECTURES were established through the generosity of a distinguished alumnus of the College of Business and Public Administration, Mr. Charles C. Moskowitz of the Class of 1914, who retired after many years as Vice President-Treasurer and a Director of Loew's Inc.

In establishing these lectures, it was Mr. Moskowitz's aim to contribute to the understanding of the function of business and its underlying disciplines in society by providing a public forum for the dissemination of enlightened business theories and practices.

The College of Business and Public Administration and New York University are deeply grateful to Mr. Moskowitz for his interest in, and contribution to, the educational and public service program of his alma mater.

This volume is the seventeenth in the Moskowitz series. The earlier ones were:

16

February, 1961 *Business Survival in the Sixties*
Thomas F. Patton, President and
Chief Executive Officer
Republic Steel Corporation

November, 1961 *The Challenges Facing Management*
Don G. Mitchell, President
General Telephone and Electronics
Corporation

November, 1962 *Competitive   Private   Enterprise
Under   Government   Regulation*
Malcolm A. MacIntyre, President
Eastern Air Lines

November, 1963 *The Common Market: Friend or
Competitor?*
Jesse W. Markham, Professor of
Economics, Princeton University
Charles E. Fiero, Vice President,
The Chase Manhattan Bank
Howard S. Piquet, Senior Specialist
in International Economics, Leg-
islative Reference Service, The
Library of Congress

November, 1964 *The Forces Influencing the American Economy*
Jules Backman, Research Professor
of Economics, New York University

> *Martin R. Gainsbrugh*, Chief Economist and Vice President, National Industrial Conference Board

November, 1965   *The American Market of the Future*
> *Arno H. Johnson*, Vice President and Senior Economist, J. Walter Thompson Company
> *Gilbert E. Jones*, President, IBM World Trade Corporation
> *Darrell B. Lucas*, Professor of Marketing and Chairman of the Department, New York University

November, 1966   *Government Wage-Price Guideposts in the American Economy*
> *George Meany*, President, American Federation of Labor and Congress of Industrial Organizations
> *Roger M. Blough*, Chairman of the Board and Chief Executive Officer, United States Steel Corporation
> *Neil H. Jacoby*, Dean, Graduate School of Business Administration, University of California at Los Angeles

November, 1967   *The Defense Sector in the American Economy*

Jacob K. Javits, United States Senator, New York

Charles J. Hitch, President, University of California

Arthur F. Burns, Chairman, Federal Reserve Board

November, 1968 *The Urban Environment: How It Can Be Improved*

William E. Zisch, Vice-chairman of the Board, Aerojet-General Corporation

Paul H. Douglas, Chairman, National Commission on Urban Problems

Professor of Economics, New School for Social Research

Robert C. Weaver, President, Bernard M. Baruch College of the City University of New York

Former Secretary of Housing and Urban Development

November, 1969 *Inflation: The Problems It Creates and the Policies It Requires*

Arthur M. Okun, Senior Fellow, The Brookings Institution

Henry H. Fowler, General Partner, Goldman, Sachs & Co.

Milton Gilbert, Economic Adviser, Bank for International Settlements

March, 1971   *The Economics of Pollution*
Kenneth E. Boulding, Professor of Economics, University of Colorado
Elvis J. Stahr, President, National Audubon Society
Solomon Fabricant, Professor of Economics, New York University
Former Director, National Bureau of Economic Research
Martin R. Gainsbrugh, Adjunct Professor of Economics, New York University
Chief Economist, National Industrial Conference Board

April, 1971   *Young America in the NOW World*
Hubert H. Humphrey, Senator from Minnesota
Former Vice President of the United States

April, 1972   *Optimum Social Welfare and Productivity: A Comparative View*
Jan Tinbergen, Professor of Development Planning, Netherlands School of Economics
Abram Bergson, George F. Baker Professor of Economics, Harvard University

Fritz Machlup, Professor of Economics, New York University

Oskar Morgenstern, Professor of Economics, New York University

April, 1973   *Fiscal Responsibility: Tax Increases of Spending Cuts?*

Paul McCracken, Edmund Ezra Day University, Professor of Business Administration, University of Michigan

Murray L. Weidenbaum, Edward Mallinckrodt Distinguished University Professor, Washington University

Lawrence S. Ritter, Professor of Finance, New York University

Robert A. Kavesh, Professor of Finance, New York University

March, 1974   *Wall Street in Transition: The Emerging System and Its Impact on the Economy*

Henry G. Manne, Distinguished Professor of Law, Director of the Center for Studies in Law and Economics, University of Miami Law School

Ezra Solomon, Dean Witter Professor of Finance, Stanford University

March, 1975   *Leaders and Followers in an Age of Ambiguity*
George P. Shultz, Professor, Graduate School of Business, Stanford University
President, Bechtel Corporation

CONTENTS

NATIONAL ECONOMIC PLANNING
METHODS AND PROBLEMS

Wassily Leontief

The notion of National Economic Planning that I have in mind is meant to encompass the entire complex of political, legislative, and administrative measures aimed at an explicit formulation and practical realization of a comprehensive national economic plan. Without a comprehensive internally consistent plan there can be, in this sense, no planning. But the preparation of a script is not enough; the play has to be staged and acted out.

It is incumbent on anyone who favors introduction of National Economic Planning in this country—and I am one of these—to propose a plan describing how this might be done. Several congressional committees and at least one commission appointed by the President, not to speak of groups outside of the government, are now engaged in this task.

1.In its published form a National Economic Plan or rather the statistical appendix to its text can be visualized as a detailed systematic annual survey of manufacture and of agriculture, of transportation, and of trade and the Federal and local budgets. However, it describes the state of the economy not—as the *Statistical Abstract* or the *Census of Manufacture* does—for one of the past years, but rather for five years in advance and in a more summary form over a much longer interval of time stretching into the future. That does not mean, however, that a plan must be rigidly adhered to over the entire period of say four or five years. On the contrary, each year the plan should be revised in the light of past experience and newly acquired information and pushed out as a moving average one year ahead.

A plan is not a forecast. The whole idea of planning assumes the possibility of choice between alternative feasible scenarios. Feasibility is the key word.

A particular national economy can and, in the context of the planning process, has to be visualized as a system consisting of mutually interdependent parts. The trucking industry must be supplied by the oil refining sector with fuel, and, to be able to expand, it must be supplied by the automobile industry with trucks, in addition to the replacement of worn out equipment. To provide employment for additional workers, the automobile industry must not only be assured of an outlet for its products, but in the long run it must construct new plants and retool the old. In the process of doing so, it has to receive from the construction industry more plant space, and from the machine-building industry additional equipment, not to speak of a greater flow of power, steel, and all the other inputs.

Traditional economic theory not only poses the problem but also explains how its solution is, or, at least, can be brought about through the operation of competitive price mechanism, that is, a trial-and-error procedure that automatically brings about in each and every market equality between supply and demand. In some markets and under certain conditions this actually works. But considering the lack of any reliable information on which to base their expectations, many business leaders have come to recognize that this trial-and-error game, instead of bringing about a desired state of stable equilibrium, results in misallocation of resources, underutilization of productive capacities, and periodic unemployment. This means lost wages, lost profits, and lost taxes; conditions that are bound to engender social unrest and sharpen the political conflict.

Conventional monetary and fiscal policies relying on a rather sketchy aggregative description and analysis of the economic system appears to be no more successful in compensating for the lack of systematic foresight, than frantic pushing and pulling out the choke is able to correct the malfunctioning and stalling of a motor. Occasionally, it works, but usually it does not.

2. The first input-output tables describing the flow of goods and services between the different sec-

tors of the American economy in census years 1919 and 1929 were published in 1936. They were based on a rather gross segregation of all economic activities in forty-four sectors. Because there were no computing facilities available for purposes of actually making analytical calculations, the sectors had to be further grouped into only ten sectors.

The data base, the computing facilities, and the analytical techniques have advanced much farther than could have been anticipated forty years ago. National input-output tables containing up to 700 distinct sectors are being compiled on a current basis, as are tables for individual, regional, state, and metropolitan areas. Private enterprise has entered the input-output business. For a fee one can now purchase a single row of a table showing the deliveries of a particular product, say, coated laminated fabrics or farming machine tools, not only to different industries, but within each industry to individual plants segregated by zip code areas.

Not that anyone could contemplate including such details in a national economic plan. Such systematic information proves to be most useful in assessing structural—in this particular instance technological—relationships between the input requirements, on the one hand, and, on the other, the levels of output of various industries: in the case of households, between total consumers' outlay and spending on each particular type of goods. Stocks of equipment, buildings, and inventories, their accumulation, their maintenance, and their occasional reduction are described and analyzed in their mutual interdependence with the flows of all kinds of goods and services throughout the entire system.

Detailed, as contrasted with aggregative, description and analysis of economic structures and relationships can, indeed, provide a suitable framework for a concrete instead of a purely symbolic description of alternative methods of production and the realistic delineation of alternative paths of technological change.

3. Choice among alternative scenarios is the clue to rational national economic planning rather than crystal-ball gazing that, with the rise of general uncertainty, became a marketable product of the economic forecasting industry. Also this is preferable to the equally fashionable, although not as profitable, preoccupation with lofty national goals.

The important practical difference in making a choice between alternative national economic plans and selecting an appropriate set of national goals can best be explained by the following example: A friend invites me for dinner in a first-class restaurant and asks that I supply him with a general description of my tastes so that he could order the food in advance. Unable to describe my—or anyone else's—tastes in general terms, I prefer to see the menu and then select, without hesitation, the combination of dishes that I like.

Confronted with alternative national economic plans—each described in great detail, particularly in respect to items that are likely to affect my own well-being and my personal assessment of equity and fairness of the whole—I would have no difficulty in deciding which of them I would prefer or, at least, consider not inferior to any other. I could do this, despite my inability to describe my preferences, my predilections, and my prejudices in general terms. A philosopher, a social psychologist, or a historian might succeed in arriving at such a generalization by inference based on interpretation of my utterances or, even better, of specific choices I have actually made before. But this, of course, is an entirely different matter.

This, I submit, is the reason why a planning process should start out not with the formulation of what theroretical economists refer to as the general "objective function,"but with elaboration of alternative scenarios each presenting in concrete, non-technical terms one of the several possible future states of the economy. The volume or a series of volumes containing such alternative scenarios would read not unlike issues of the *United States Statistical Abstract* with sections devoted to Industrial Production, to Agriculture, to Trade and Transportation, to Consumption, to Medical Services, to Education, and so on not only on a national but also on regional and even local levels.

Karl Marx would have rejected this as an utopian approach and so do the libertarian opponents of national economic planning. Both view the concrete shape of the unknown future as unfolding itself while time marches on. The only difference between these two believers in the "invisible hand" is that the latter is ready to accept and approve whatever might come, provided it has not been planned, while the former is convinced that, while unpredictable in all particulars, the path inevitably leads to violent collapse of the present social and economic order.

4. To repeat: Public discussion and democratic choice among the available alternatives will be possible only if each of them is presented in concrete tangible details rather than in such summary terms as the per capital GNP, the average rate of unemployment, or the annual rate of growth of the "implicit price deflator."

The technical apparatus we would require in order to project such detailed realistic images is bound to be quite intricate and very costly, as is the inside of a television set. When it comes to preparation of a national economic plan, no effort should be spared in making use of the most dependable data-gathering and data-handling techniques and of the most advanced economic model-building and computational procedures.

The programs of the principal Federal statistical agencies will have to be greatly strengthened and, in some instances, overhauled. Much of the needed additional information can be obtained not through official questionnaires, but by means of more sophisticated methods successfully employed in commercial market research and with the help of specialized private data-gathering organizations.

Most of the economic forecasters develop their projections in such aggregative terms that relevant details pertaining, for example, to anticipated technical change are either disregarded at the outset or get dissipated in the ascent (or should I say descent?) from concrete engineering details to the formation of representative indices or broad statistical aggregates.

The data-gatherers and model-builders involved in the planning process will have to break down the barrier that separates economists, in particular academic economists, from experts possessing specialized technical knowledge of various fields of production and consumption, as well as of private and public management.

Alternative scenarios can be expected to differ from each other mainly in the extent to which the available economic resources are apportioned for private and public use and, in the case of the public use, whether more or less of the resources are allocated, to the satisfaction of this or that category of pressing needs. The scenarios will incorporate alternative policy proposals concerning energy, environment, or, say, foreign aid and national defense. To the extent to which resource availability and even the fundamental consumption patterns of various types of households are not overly affected by a shift from one scenario to another—however different they may be in their political economic and social implications—such shift will involve the use of essentially the same analytical formulation and of the same data base.

5. The internal setup of the organization responsible for preparation of alternative scenarios, elaboration of the national economic plan, and its subsequent revisions has to be dictated by requirements of its technical, nonpolitical task. One

can visualize it as an autonomous public body loosely connected with the Executive branch of the Federal Government. Eventually, it should be linked with its counterparts in the fifty states and possibly some large metropolitan areas.

The final version of the *national economic plan* will be an end product of the typically American political logrolling and legislative wrangles. The stand-by role of the technical organization referred to above will consist in seeing that, through all its transformation from the first to the last, the overall plan retains its integrity: Do not allocate more than you can produce, but also see to it that nothing is left over (unemployment is labor that is left over!).

6. However intricate the process of drawing up the blue-print of the building, the task of actual construction poses a still greater challenge.

To try to describe systematically and in full detail the array of measures to be used for purposes of practical implementation of the first national economic plan would be as futile as an attempt to trace in advance the route that Lewis and Clark followed on their way to the mouth of the Columbia River. I will take up, however, one by one, some questions that have been raised about the practical possibilities of introducing national economic planning in this country.

In abstract, one could imagine a self-fulfilling plan that would be acted out without any prompting on the economic stage, once the script has been explained. Practically, this is an impossibility. However, if the main characters can be induced, in one way or another, to play their parts, the rest of the cast can be expected to join in spontaneously. Once, for example, a decision has been made and necessary capital has been provided, in compliance with the plan, to proceed with construction of a new fertilizer plant, equipment manufacturers, building contractors, and other suppliers will fall over each other to provide the necessary structures, machinery, and all the other inputs. The force propelling them will be, of course, the profit motive operating through the automatic supply-demand mechanism. As a matter of fact, that force and that mechanism can be expected to operate particularly well if, in accordance with provisions of the national plan, the availability of energy, labor, and all other inputs will be secured in required amounts in the right place at the right time. In a planned economy the price mechanism will be an effective but humble servant of the society not, as it often is, an overbearing and all too often fumbling master.

In the example given above, the point of direct, as contrasted to indirect, enforcement of a plan was the decision to expand the productive capacities of particular sectors. The specific means used in this case might have been selective control of capital and credit flows, tax exemption, or even direct public investment.

The selection of strategically commanding points in which to apply direct influence or control as well as choice of the method or of a combination of methods to be applied in each point to bring about compliance with the plan has to be based on the concrete study of the specific configuration of economic flow. The analogy with the tasks of a hydraulic engineer charged with regulating a major water system is more than superficial. Dams, dikes, and occasional locks have to be placed so we can take advantage of the natural flow propelled by gravity (the profit motive) but at the same time permit us to eliminate floods and devastating droughts.

Considering the great variety of ways and the extent to which the government now affects the operation of the economy of the United States, one of our lesser worries should be the lack of the accelerating, breaking, or steering devices that could be used to guide it smoothly and securely along a chosen path. The real trouble is that, at the present, the government not only does not know what road it wants to follow but does not even have a map. To make things worse, one member of the crew in charge presses down the accelerator, another pumps the brakes, a third turns the wheel, and the fourth sounds the horn. Is that the way to reach your destination safely?

7. These observations, naturally, lead to the question of planning within the Federal Government itself; charity should begin at home. The recent establishment of orderly budgetary procedures is a move in the right direction, but it only scratches the surface of the problem.

Consider, for example, the lack of effective coordination between our environmental and our energy policies. Each is controlled by a different department, not to speak of many smaller, often semiautonomous, agencies. Production of fuel and generation of energy is one of the principle sources of pollution. Any major move in the field of energy can be expected to have far-reaching effects on the environment, and vice versa! The energy-producing industry is immediately and directly affected by anti-pollution regulations. The obvious practical step to take to solve this problem is for both agencies to combine their data banks (their stocks of factual information) and to agree to base their policy decisions on a common model. This model should be capable of generating scenarios displaying jointly the energy and the environmental reprecussions of any move that either one of the two agencies might contemplate making. Adversary policy debate could and should continue, but adversary fact finding would have become impossible, and policies that tend to cancel out or contradict each other would at least be shown up for what they are.

But, why should not one include the railway industry, the air and highway transport in the same picture? These sectors, after all, not only use fuel but also move it and discharge pollutants unless precautionary measures have been taken. Indeed, why not? Particularly, if that could induce the semi-independent agencies concerned with the regulation of these sectors to coordinate their action with those of the ERDA and the EPA. But this leads directly to national planning; yes, indeed, it does.

While monetary and fiscal measures have for years served as instruments of economic policy planning, the nearly exclusive reliance on these two tools, under the influence of the Keynesian, and perhaps I should add Friedmanian, doctrines, can hardly be justified by the results attained. Other means of keeping the economy on the right course must come into their own.

8. This has immediate bearing on the problem of inflation. The fact that the labor unions, while concerned with real wages, can bargain only for money wages is a major, possibly *the* major, factor contributing to perpetuation of the inflationary spiral. General wage and price controls, without supporting national planning action, are bound in the long run, to bring about cumulative distortions in the allocation and utilization of economic resources. Within the framework of an effectively conceived planning action they would become unnecessary and eventually obsolete. By offering the leadership of the labor unions the opportunity to take a responsible and effective part in the design and implementation of a national economic plan, the power of organized labor, instead of being dissipated or absorbed by inflation, would thus be applied where it counts.

I see no reason to assume that the introduction of national economic planning would require or could bring about a marked shift in the overall national balance of economic and political power. The wealthy with the support of their retainers can be expected to continue to rule the roost. The inner workings of the system would, however, become more transparent. By comparing scenarios prepared in conformity with Mr. Reagan's or President Ford's ideas and those constructed in conformity with Senator Humphrey's and Senator Udall's specifications, the American citizen would find it easier to make a rational choice.

PLANNING THE ECONOMY

Herbert Stein

I will stipulate at the outset that many people are unhappy about the performance of the American economy. This unhappiness is not confined to editorial writers and professors. Many ordinary, nonintellectual people share it.

The fact of this unhappiness, or even the fact that this unhappiness is greater than in the past, tells us little about the American economy. It is in the nature of the world that people should be unhappy about their economy unless they are either extraordinarily sophisticated or extraordinarily complacent. We live in a world of scarcity, and all an economic system can do is organize that scarcity to make the best of it. An economic system cannot deliver everything that people want. That is why economics is called the dismal science.

Once people start evaluating the economy in which they live they are bound to be disappointed and unhappy unless they have some standard of achievement other than the fulfillment of all their wishes. They need some standard of what is reasonably expectable, which might be provided by a comparison with other countries and other times. But few people have such a standard, and those who do don't say much about it. So the common unhappiness is not necessarily a reflection on the adequacy of the economic system.

Even if this is granted, the unhappiness is itself a real fact, and an important one. At a press conference in 1973 I was trying to explain that although people were terribly anxious and unhappy about the inflation there was no evidence that it had, up to then, impaired their real incomes. One of the reporters then asked me why we cared about the inflation, if real incomes were unimpaired. I replied that, contrary to common belief, we thought it a bad thing for a large part of the population to be unhappy, even if that unhappiness had no further consequences.

However, it is not part of my purpose here today to discuss ways of curing unhappiness that does not result from inadequate performance of the economy.

I will further stipulate that the economy is not working as well as it might, or as we might reasonably expect. I am not absolutely sure that is true, but it seems to me to have sufficient probability of being true to justify the investment of considerable effort to discover whether we can find ways to make it work better. So I am not going to defend the proposition that this is the best of all possible worlds. The problem is to find in what respects the economic performance is deficient, and why, and by what means it can be improved.

The specific problem is to discover whether and how something called economic planning can contribute to making the economy work better. It is necessary to use the vague term "something called economic planning" because the most obvious feature of the discussion of economic planning is that the term has no specific meaning. The discussion is either about what it is or is totally confused by failure to say what it is.

People are expressing several attitudes toward economic planning today. There are some people who are against it, whatever it is. There are some people who are for it, whatever it is. There are some people who are for it and are willing to let you define it any way you like—that is, any way that would make you agree to be for it also. And there are people who are for it on some definitions and against it on others.

I consider myself to be a member of the last group. I favor planning on some definitions of it and oppose it on others. I also oppose undefined planning because I believe that if we authorize something called planning without defining it, the ordinary processes of government and politics will move it towards kinds of planning I dislike. Indeed, I consider that one of the great dangers—not that legislation will be passed explicitly to inaugurate a massive system of detailed control over the American economy but that Congress will unwittingly write a blank check which will tend to the same result in the end.

Possible meanings of the term economic planning, as used by some of its advocates or at least involved in the discussion, may be classified in the following way. All of them are statements of what government should do.

First, some people who propose planning are only proposing that government should do what it already does, and has done for a long time. In a recent article in the *New York Times Magazine*, Robert Heilbroner argues that the United States will and should embrace economic planning. He then gives as one example of what that might mean that the government might have a plan to check inflation. It is only possible to think that the government does not have a plan to check inflation if one makes the mistake, common to planners, of confusing a plan to achieve a certain objective with the achievement of the objective. On that basis one might conclude that since we have not checked inflation we have not had a plan to do so. I can testify that what Mark Twain said about stopping smoking is also true about planning to stop inflation. He said it wasn't hard to stop smoking. He had done it dozens of times.

In general, one can say that advocates of planning are quite ignorant of the number of subjects on which the government makes forecasts and plans, even long-term ones. They do not recognize that the government does this because they see little result from the forecasts and plans. But this should raise a question in their minds about whether having plans, or a plan, is the vital missing ingredient for solving the nation's economic problems.

A second meaning of planning is that the government should carry out the functions which it is now recognized to have, and which it is attempting to discharge, but should do them better. There should be more information, more analysis, a longer view, and more objective evaluation of costs and benefits.

A third meaning might be regarded as an aspect of the second, but it is so often mentioned separately that it deserves a number of its own. That is the coordination of the economic activities of government. Senator Humphrey, who is, of course, a chief sponsor of legislation embodying the idea of planning, regularly complains that government's right hand does not know what the left hand is doing. Humphrey's complaint is a common theme among advocates of planning, which is supposed to correct that difficulty.

A fourth idea that some people seem to have in mind when they propose economic planning is simply that the government should provide some particular benefit. As far as I can determine from the statements of Senator Javits, the other chief sponsor of the bill, this is his primary interest. In addition to wanting the government to be more rational—something we presumably all want—he wants the government to pay for some specific services, such as health insurance, and thinks that a planning system will get those particular decisions made.

A fifth possible meaning of planning is that the government should exercise control over some particular aspect of economic life, like the purity of the air or the conservation of energy. Many arguments for planning consist of statements of the need for government intervention in one or more of such cases.

Sixth, there is the notion that the government should develop a comprehensive, and fairly detailed, plan for the performance of the economy for some years into the future. They expect that the existence and publication of the plan itself would influence behavior to conform to the plan. No other forms of control or coercion would be needed. The degree of detail, and the range of variables to be covered by the plan, are critical for evaluating the significance of this notion, and sponsors have not been specific about this. Of course, it must be understood that the degree of detail is finer than the categories for which the government now has objectives and plans, such as total real output, total employment and unemployment, the movement of the Consumers' Price Index and possibly some other price indices. In earlier days one might have included the balance of payments in this list.

The essence of the sixth version of planning is that the government would have plans and objectives going far beyond these gross aggregates to cover a considerable amount of sectoral and industrial detail. In the few cases where examples are given, the automobile industry is the sector most commonly cited. I suppose at a minimum the planners are talking about thirty to eighty industrial sectors—thirty being the number for which monthly payroll figures are published by the Bureau of Labor Statistics and eighty being the number for which annual income figures are published by the Bureau of Economic Analysis. For each of these sectors, presumably, the plan would specify some measure of output, investment, employment, possible inventories, possibly some measure of prices.

Since the modern discussion of planning puts a great deal of emphasis on "regional balance," presumably the plan would specify the key variable for each industrial sector for each region, as well as the national total. How numerous are the regions among which balance is to be achieved is another subject on which the planners are silent. Are we talking about balance among the twelve Federal Reserve districts, among the fifty states, or among several hundred standard metropolitan statistical areas?

Also, since the discussion puts a great deal of weight on "long-run" planning, one must assume that the plan would specify goals for each of the next five years.

When all of these dimensions are added together, or multiplied together, the plan is seen to consist of something between about 5000 target numbers and possibly 100,000 or even 400,000 numbers.

What distinguishes this sixth version of planning from the seventh and eighth to which I will soon come is that no form of control or coercion is intended. Of course, the advocates of planning wish that private behavior would conform to the plan, but they expect that the development and publication of the plan would bring that conformity about. Each private actor would see that the plan is logical and rational. Moreover, he would expect that all others would conform to the plan, and as a consequence he would find it in his interest also to conform to it. One

point on which advocates of planning are usually explicit is that they do not intend that the plan should
specify the behavior of any particular individual or
company, even a very large company. The plan might
specify production and investment in the automobile
industry, but it would not specify production and investment by General Motors.

This sixth version of planning is modelled on
what French planning is supposed to have been like
in the 1950's. That was called indicative planning, to
suggest that the planning authorities only indicated
the way the economy should go, and the various ac-
tors in the drama played out their roles without any
compulsion. In fact, French planning, even when it
was operational, was not like that. It was much closer
to the seventh version of planning in my list.

The seventh version of planning itself might take
the form I have described in version six, but there
would be a more active effort to assure conformity to
the plan. This effort would not ordinarily consist of a
direct government mandate. Conforming might be
assured by applying a selective tax incentive or sub-
sidy, or allocating credit, or distributing government
contracts, addressing moral suasion to particular
businesses, or distributing praise and criticism.
Presumably these means would not be used to bring
about conformity with every one of the many
thousand dimensions of the plan. The dimensions
could be divided into three categories: those that
would be spontaneously met, those that might not be
met but the nonconformity of which the authorities
felt able to disregard, and those that the authorities
felt had to be conformed to.

Not to prolong this catalog unduly, my final and eighth version of planning might be called Stalinist planning. The plan itself would not necessarily depart importantly from the plan described in versions six or seven. However, the government would command conformity with the plan, and this would require specifying and ordering the performance of individuals, not just of sectors. Probably, even in a Stalinist system, achievement of all the plan targets would not be demanded with equal rigor. Some slippages might be tolerated.

I do not propose to discuss all of these possible meanings of economic planning. Some do not deserve discussion at all. There is no point to discussing a proposal, made as a great innovation and based on ignorance, that the government should do something that it is already doing and has been doing for a long time. Neither is it possible in this space, or profitable, to discuss any or all of the specific benefit provisions or economic controls that various people are advocating and calling planning. Each of these specific proposals has its own rationale, its own costs and benefits to be appraised, and one cannot make any general statement about them. Certainly I do not want to be in the position of saying that there is no possible new form of government intervention that might be desirable, any more than I would say that all present kinds of government intervention need to be continued. However, I do not think that all specific forms of intervention now being imposed or possible new ones can be fruitfully discussed under the general heading of planning. The discussion of planning as a comprehensive system for organizing the economy is nevertheless relevant to the consideration of specific intervention and programs. As Jewkes once said, to discuss each case on its merits is not to discuss the merits of the case. The proliferation of specific kinds of intervention, each of them justified in its own terms as an exception to the general system, may add up to a change in the general system that was not intended or wanted. Or the proliferation of the specific types of intervention may so weaken the market economy that a workable system can only be created by proceeding on to a more comprehensive planning system. So the case against general comprehensive planning is, in my opinion, an argument, although not a conclusive argument in any particular case, against making further specific intervention.

We can also rule out as not worth discussion what I have called the Stalinist verson of planning. None of the present advocates of planning in the United States, as far as I can see, proposes a total command system. The only reason we might consider that kind of system is whether it is in fact the result, even though undesired, of starting along the path of the other, softer versions of planning.

So what I am left with is, on the one hand, planning as meaning the improvement of the processes by which the government performs its present and well-established functions, and, on the other hand, planning as meaning the comprehensive specification of the desirable performance of numerous sectors of the economy, going well beyond the present scale of government intervention, but not intended to involve complete and mandatory control. The second of these is what I understand to be the aim of the current interest in planning, which has found its most concrete expression in the Balanced Economic Growth Bill sponsored by Senators Humphrey and Javits and others. I shall discuss this version of planning first, and then return to the possible content of the other general idea, that is, the improvement of the performance of the existing economic functions of government.

The rationale of the current planning proposals is best understood by contrasting it with the view of the role of government in the economy which had become standard in the preceding forty years. This view was shared by the leading schools of economics during that period, by fiscalists and monetarists, Keynesians and Friedmanites. It was obviously not a view which denied a crucial role and responsibility to government, but it was at the same time a view which assigned key functions to the free market. In my mind the philosophy was best summed up in the title of Henry Simon's important essay, "A Positive Program for Laissez-Faire."

In this view the government had responsibility for maintaining economic stability. There were differences of opinion among subscribers to this view about whether this stability should be measured by the steadiness of the rate of growth of nominal demand, or of total output, or by a certain unemployment rate, or by the stability of some overall measure of average prices. But the essential point is that the target was some great aggregate. Moreover, the target was to be achieved by some combination of fiscal and monetary measures which would be general in their impact. Of course, these measures would not affect every individual or economic sector equally, but the differences would not be the object of the policy.

The government would also have responsibility for affecting the distribution of income, to make it more equal, or to keep individuals or families from falling below some socially acceptable level. We would have to decide how far to go in this respect by means of the democratic process. The philosophy itself did not answer that question, and different people who shared the consensus would have answered it differently.

In this view the government would be responsible for providing some services whose benefits could not be divided up and assessed to individuals to pay for. National defense was the most obvious example, but what we now call protection of the environment would also fall in that category. However, the total fraction of the national income that would be spent on this category would be small. Government would also have the function of maintaining competition, and possibly in rare cases where that was impossible or uneconomical, of regulating prices.

This view of the role of government in the economy might have sprung full-blown from the brow of Adam Smith. However, the consensus of the past forty years constituted a reaffirmation of this view after a period of challenge. The main challenge came in the early days of the Great Depression, when there was much thrashing around to try to determine what was wrong with the economy. Many people, including many businessmen, believed that there was a fundamental structural defect in the system which required the kind of intervention in the details of the economic system that was incorporated in the National Recovery Act. This was also a period when economic planning as practiced in the Soviet Union, in Fascist Italy, and in Nazi Germany was regarded by some as a model for us.

The reaffirmation of the conservative consensus on the role of government after the mid-1930's resulted from a combination of factors. Planning as practiced, for example by the NRA, was seen to be irrelevant to the solution of the Depression, as well as unconstitutional. Keynes, although considered a radical by many, focussed attention again on a macroeconomic approach to economic problems, that is, on an approach using general fiscal-monetary policy to deal with aggregate demand. Moreover, the Soviet, Italian, and German planning systems were seen to be connected with an intolerable repression of individual freedom.

This standard view of the function of government in the economy was that the government would maintain a framework of overall stability, would moderate economic inequality, and would maintain competition, and within that framework the free market would determine what got produced, in response to consumers' demands, and how things got produced, under competitive pressure for efficiency. This division of labor between government and the market promised not only efficiency but also freedom. Although the government would have a big and powerful role, its influence would be general. It could not reward or punish particular individuals and thus force them to behave as the government wanted them to behave.

The new advocacy of planning implies a different view of the role of government and rests on a different view of what the economic problem is. This view of the economic problem may be called "radical chic," since, in my opinion, its raison d'etre is the desire to be fashionable and "different" and to distinguish oneself from what economists have been thinking for 200 years. The basic element in the radical chic view is that the market no longer serves to guide the economy efficiently. Several reasons are alleged for thinking that.

One is the proposition that the degree of competition in the modern economy is very low, presumably much lower than it was in some earlier golden age. One aspect of that, apparently, is the spread of the multinational corporation. Indeed, "multinational corporation" is one of the favorite buzzwords of radical chic economics. Again, what is the significance of the existence of multinational corporations has never been clearly explained, but it is a term which seems to terrorize people. Presumably what is implied is that the multinational corporation escapes the discipline of the market while also escaping the discipline of national governments.

Other allegations about the inadequacy of the market to guide economic affairs revolve around the belief that the world, or at least the industrial world, is getting poorer, or will not continue to get rich as fast as it has in the past two centuries. That is due to the fact that we are running out of things, specifically natural resources. Related to that is the belief that the less-developed countries, where many natural resources come from, are going to be more demanding about their share of the world's income, and more aggressive in using their economic power to extract a larger share from us. The oil situation is the obvious model for this.

This change in the world's material situation is supposed to call for more national economic planning for several reasons. First, while the market may have been a satisfactory instrument for managing our affairs while we were becoming richer, we can no longer afford the luxury of the free market while we are becoming poorer. Second, the involvement of foreign governments, or cartels in the markets for raw materials introduces an unpredictability with which private businesses cannot cope. Third, it becomes necessary to deal with foreign governments, and only the government at home can do that. Fourth, private individuals and businesses do not have the motivation to consider the interests of future generations in preserving the supply of depletable resources.

This concern about the supply of raw materials is an absolutely key factor in the thinking of many advocates of planning. For example, Mr. Leonard Woodcock, who is Co-Chairman of the Initiative Committee for National Economic Planning, has said that it was the world oil problem which convinced him of the need for planning. In the spring of 1974 Senators Mansfield and Scott, Majority and Minority Leaders of the Senate, wrote to President Nixon expressing their fundamental doubts about the adequacy of the nation's economic system. The President sent several of his economic officials up to the Capitol to learn what the Senators had in mind and it turned out that they believed that existing free-market systems were inadequate to deal with the problem of materials supply, especially as the supplies were of foreign origin. One upshot of this concern was the establishment of a new commission which will study, among other things, the need for comprehensive economic planning.

Another ingredient in the radical chic view of the world which gives rise to the call for planning is the belief that the economy has become enormously more complex than it used to be, so that we can no longer rely upon the invisible hand to take care of it. Closely related to it is the idea that the whole economic system is overrun with what economists call externalities, or situations in which private decision makers do not feel either the full benefits or the full costs of their decisions and therefore do not adequately take these costs and benefits into account.

While all these views about the state of the economy are commonly held and expressed, the evidence for them is most unimpressive. Many studies have been made of the degree of competition, monopoly, and market concentration in the economy today. There is no evidence to lead us to believe that the degree of competition is now lower than it was, say, in 1890. There are larger corporations, but the whole economy is much larger. The reduction of barriers to international trade and the much greater mobility of goods, capital, and information within and between countries have increased effective competition greatly.

The complaints about the multinational corporations are particularly unfounded. The chief significance of the multinational corporation is that it improves the freedom of movement of resources, technology, and capital around the world. Multinational corporations are subject to the national laws of the places where they operate. They only escape national control in the sense that all international trade escapes national control. If one country makes the production of chocolate candy within its borders unprofitable, then chocolate candy will be produced elsewhere, whether or not there are multinational corporations in the business: in this sense the production of chocolate candy will have escaped national control.

As for the claim that the world is getting poorer and running out of resources, that is groundless also. Of course, we have been using up specific nonreplaceable resources since the year one. But the investment of savings and talent in the accumulation of capital, technical knowledge, and the skills of the labor force has increased the world's productive capacity much more than the using up of natural resources has reduced it. In fact, investment and research has greatly increased the amount of the world's natural resources that is economically usable. After all, one hundred years ago petroleum that was under 1500 feet of ocean might just as well not have been there, as far as the world economy was concerned. There is little basis for the view that the less-developed countries are going to cartellize the supply of natural resources and extract a price from the industrial countries which will significantly change the conditions of economic life here. For various reasons, the oil situation is unique and will not be repeated with other resources, however aggressive the demands of the less-developed countries may be.

Neither is it correct to argue that the private market contains no mechanism for bringing about the conservation of depletable resources. Any private party who has property rights in depletable resources must make a decision between using the resources now and holding them for the future. In making that decision he compares the price he can get for the resources today with the price he might get for them later. The more likely they are to be scarce in the future the greater the future price is likely to be relative to the present price and the stronger his incentive to hold the resources for the future. If this process did not work, we would have run out of a lot of things before now. And there is no reason to think that this process does not adequately represent the interests of both the present and future generations in the use of the limited resource. There are well-known cases in which individuals do not have exclusive property rights to the depletable resource, like ocean fisheries or common grazing lands, and where the private system would lead to overuse. These cases are, however, exceptional.

One should probably recognize that the control of some natural resources by foreign governments introduces an element of uncertainty with which private enterprises find it difficult to deal. But government planners will find that condition difficult to

deal with also. Although the United States Government has been involved in the oil-supply question for
many years, and conducted an exhaustive study of oil
imports as late as 1970, it did not foresee the formation of the cartel only two years later. In fact, it
explicitly dismissed the possibility. And none of the
other countries that have planning systems did any
better in foreseeing the big change in the world oil
situation before it happened or adapting to it after it
happened.

In general, we can see that real world economies
will be exposed to surprises and potential disrup-
tions. However, widening the range of government
responsibility is not likely to reduce such surprises or
their disruptive consequences. In fact, probably
nothing in recent years has caused so much uncertainty in the economy as the economic policy of
our own government. This became very clear when
we had the price controls of 1971 to 1974, which was
as close to a comprehensive economic planning
system as we have had in peacetime since 1935.

Finally, in this review of the elements of the
radical chic view of the economy, it is probably
correct that the economy is becoming more complex
in the sense that the number of connections between
one person and one decision and another is becoming
greater. This is a natural consequence of the in-
creasing division of labor that comes with the ex-
pansion of markets and increase of affluence.
However, the notion that this calls for more planning
begs the central question and is, indeed, the opposite
of the truth. The more complex the interrelationships
the less effectively they can be comprehended by a

single, centralized planning agency in Washington
and the greater the need to rely on a decentralized
system, which is what the free market is.

Thus, in my view, the new description of the
economic condition which is used to demonstrate the
inadequacy of the standard view of the appropriate
relations between the government and the economy is
largely wrong, and insofar as it does reflect real
changes in the national or world economy those are
not changes which call for a comprehensive economic
planning system. I would like to pass on now to a
consideration of what the planning proposals offer
us, and what the chances are that planning would
deliver on its promises.

Probably the most surprising aspect of the
current discussion on economic planning is the
vagueness of the goals which the planning is to serve.
This is most surprising because advocates of planning
are so emphatic about the need for rationality, which
seems to imply the need to start with a clear
specification of objectives and then to proceed with
the fashioning of procedures and policies for
achieving the objectives. But the current planning
proposals are long on procedures but short on both
policies and objectives, unless you consider "To do
better" a useful statement of an objective.

The Humphrey-Javits Bill is the most-developed
formulation of what today's planners have in mind,
and it may be used as an example. It gives us a list of
areas in which we are to have goals, or subjects about
which we are to have goals, but it does not tell us
what the goals are to be. The list is highly revealing,
and I quote it here:

The Plan shall—

(1) establish economic objectives for a period to be determined by the (Economic Planning) Board, paying particular attention to the attainment of the goals of full employment, price stability, balanced economic growth, an equitable distribution of income, the efficient utilization of both private and public resources, balanced regional and urban development, stable international relations, and meeting essential national needs in transportation, energy, agriculture, raw materials, housing, education, public services, and research and development.

These are clearly not operational goals for a plan. They are not sufficiently specific or quantitative to provide a starting point for drawing up programs. If this is not self-evident, one only needs to ask himself what "balanced economic growth" is. The proponents of planning regard this as a key goal. They call their bill the Balanced Economic Growth and Planning Act. But they have not defined it in any way, not explained what is to be balanced, or what constitutes balance conceptually, let alone tried to assign any numbers to "balance." The same comments apply to almost all the items in the list of subjects about which we are to have goals. Even "full employment," probably the most traditional of all the areas listed, raises numerous questions of definition and measurement.

However, one should not conclude that this listing of areas of interest is innocuous because it is vague. In fact, the list gives an idea of how far the planners intend to go in spreading the influence of government.

I can hear Senator Humphrey saying that the list is merely a recital of the things that everyone is interested in and asking if I do not care about balanced economic growth, and efficient utilization of resources, and meeting essential needs for this and that. The answer is that I do care, but that I do not regard the government as the only instrument through which the people of the United States can describe and achieve their goals. The implication of the proposed planning legislation is that the government has the responsibility for saying what our goals are, and for taking steps to achieve them, in an enormous and unlimited part of our lives.

There are, in my opinion, two reasons for the vagueness with which the advocates of planning describe the goals of the plan. One is that it is intellectually difficult to be more specific. As soon as one tries to put more content and measurement into these big words, problems appear. The second reason is that it is politically suicidal to be more specific. That is, if the advocates of planning specified what they meant by, for example, balanced growth or equitable distribution of income, many people who think they are in favor of planning would find that they are going to get less out of it than they had expected. Support for the idea would fall off rapidly during the controversy that surely would arise over who was to be its beneficiary.

While advocates of planning naturally imply that their proposed system would identify and serve the important interests of the American people, their more explicit claim is that planning will be more efficient than the unguided market system in achieving whatever goals the process is aimed at. Even if true this might be considered a mixed blessing. If the system aims at a set of goals chosen by some mixture of bureaucrats and politicians, the inefficiency of the system may be our salvation.

One would have thought that by now there would no longer be any question about the superiority of the market over centralized planning as a way of organizing an economic system—abstracting now from the question of goals. The heliotropic striving of the planned economies of Eastern Europe towards a price and market system ought to be important evidence. In addition there has been a large amount of convincing economic analysis.

The question is how best to bring to bear upon economic decisions the near-infinity of bits of knowledge that is relevant to choosing which of millions of possible products should be produced, in what amounts, by what techniques, and with what inputs, where and for whom. The relevant information is now widely dispersed among millions of individuals who know what the production possibilities they face are and what their own preferences are. To make sensible economic decisions, all of these bits of information need to be integrated. The automobile producer knows how to make an engine block out of either cast iron or aluminum. Before he can make a rational decision on which to use, he needs information about the supply conditions of the two materials, about all their alternative uses, and about the preferences of consumers.

There are two ways in which this great mass of outside information can be combined with the information that each actor in the process starts with. All of the information can be funnelled into the central planning agency which would manipulate it to reach a decision. Or, the information can be synthesized by a market process which boils it down to the minimum requirements of each decision. For example, the automobile manufacturer does not have to know what all the competing uses of iron and aluminum are. He only needs to observe the prices of the two materials in the market, which summarize all that information. Also consumers' preferences are revealed to him by the prices that they are willing to pay for the two kinds of automobiles.

Even with the marvels of the computer there is no way to replicate this market process, let alone improve on it, by relying on the collection of statistics and their central manipulation. All we have been able to do in the way of collecting statistics is to assemble gross, unreliable, and belated information on what the market has done. The categories, and even the categories we can conceive of, are too crude for deciding what, how, and for whom to produce. They only tell us what choices the market made, not what choices were open to be made, and therefore, they provide no basis for deciding that some other choice would have been better. They refer to the past, whereas decision making requires constant adaptation to a rapidly changing environment.

This issue was definitely discussed in an article

by Professor von Hayek entitled "The Use of Knowledge in Society," first published in the *American Economic Review* in 1945. He has recently restated the analysis in the *Morgan Guaranty Survey*. Everyone interested in the subject of national economic planning should read these articles. The general point is that as an instrument for assimilating and applying the knowledge relevant to organizing an economic system planning bears the same relation to the market as an amoeba bears to the human brain.

Discussion of economic planning is confused by repeated use of analogies in which a single objective exists or is to be chosen and there is either only one way to achieve the objective or the choice of ways does not matter. A piano is to be moved, and it can only be moved if five men cooperate. Four men are in an automobile, and if they are to go anywhere they are all to go the same place. A man is to be put on the moon, and we do not care how much it costs. In those cases all that is needed is a plan or a directive.

But the social-economic problem is much different from that. It is how to reconcile the objectives of 215 million different people with respect to the production and distribution of millions of goods and services when the objectives and the conditions of production are in constant and unforeseeable flux. The reconciliation must be satisfactory to the 215 million, not just to planners in Washington. The problem is not solved by a "democratic" choice among alternative plans. The alternative plans, necessarily quite limited in number, would have to be selected by a small bureaucracy and a choice among them would have to be made by some other relatively small body, like the Congress or, more realistically, by a few Congressional leaders and Staff. But even if the decision makers in government are assumed to be fully representative, they can only represent the majority of the people, and the plan will be coercive to the minority. And, given the small number of options among which the government can practically choose, the outcome is almost certain to be less satisfactory in many respects to the majority than would be possible if all private individuals could make whatever arrangements among themselves they found to be mutually beneficial.

Faith in national economic planning rests upon a naive view of what the economic policy problem is. It regards the problem as one of combining a body of available information in a way that will objectively determine what appropriate policy should be, and that will be universally recognized as appropriate policy once the calculations are done. All that is needed, in this view, is enough scientific economists in white smocks putting the data into enough computers.

But that is not the problem at all. It is not a lack of economists and computers that keeps us from forming good economic policy. The problem is ignorance and interest. We, economists, do not know enough to tell public officials and the public at large with much confidence or precision what the consequences of alternative policies would be. Moreover, given what information and analysis experts have been able to supply, policy decisions have been too much dominated by special interests as against general interests and by short-run interests as against long-run interests.

These deficiences are not going to be corrected by planning. There is a cliché about computers which says: Garbage in, garbage out. If you put into the computer erroneous data and invalid relations you will not get good answers out, no matter how powerful the computer. And if you put into the economic planning process ignorance about the economy, and the dominance of special interests, you will not get good economic policy out, no matter how elaborate the economic planning mechanism.

Our great need today is not to broaden the part of our lives which is influenced or dominated by that highly imperfect instrument, government economic policy. Our great need is to try to make economic policy better in that limited but still important area where the government's participation is indispensable. Specifically, we need to devote ourselves to the improvement of public policy for stabilizing the economy.

The great failure of economic performance in the past decade has been the high and accelerating inflation, which culminated in the worst recession of the postwar period. This failure occured despite general acceptance of the responsibility of government for the maintenance of high employment and price stability. It occured despite unquestioned government control of the basic instruments for carrying out that responsibility, namely, fiscal and monetary policy. And it occured despite the existence of adequate machinery, at least in the Administration and the Federal Reserve, for planning and executing policy.

There were two reasons for the failure. First, economists did not know enough. We did not accurately forecast the inflation and we did not accurately predict the extent and duration of the fiscal and monetary restraint needed to check the inflation and avoid the cruel choice between unemployment and inflation that we now face. The limitation of what economists knew left a range of uncertainty about the policy that would be appropriate for economic stabilization. Second, within the range of choices that were open in the face of the uncertainty left by the diagnosis and the prescriptions of economists, policy makers too often chose what turned out to be the inflationary course. In doing this they were responding to the public demand for high employment, for easy money, for large government expenditures, and for avoiding tax increases.

These deficiencies will not be easily overcome. However, some suggestions can be offered with respect to the means we might take to solve the problem of ignorance, which is partly a problem of not knowing accurately what has been happening in the economy. That is, it is a problem of the inadequacy of statistics. There have been a number of occasions in the past ten years when those who were making economic policy were seriously misled by the unreliability of the basic data. We did not know, for example, how close we were to capacity operations in many industries at the beginning of 1973. A year later we were quite ignorant of the true state of business inventories. We have not learned enough about the characteristics of unemployment and the unemployed to understand their causes or appraise their consequences adequately. And these are only a few obvious examples.

Economic statistics could be greatly improved by the application of more money and talent to the task. I believe that would be eminently worthwhile. One of the few good results I see from the current interest in economic planning is that it focusses attention on the need for more and better economic data.

However, even if we improve the data, it will only go a little way toward improving our understanding of the economy. We are, it seems, more in the dark about the underlying macroeconomic relations than we have been, or have known we were, for a long time. For example, the relation between the money supply and the national income has come completely unstuck. Estimates of the size of the multipliers of government expenditures made by econometric techniques by investigators with similar theoretical backgrounds differ substantially. We are far from having any reliable understanding of the relation between the behavior of real output and the behavior of the average level of prices.

Obviously, we cannot order up solutions to problems that have defied economists for two centuries. However, the process of learning some of the things we need to know might be speeded up by concentrating a greater amount of the economists' research efforts on the critical problem areas. The government could contribute to this, financially and otherwise. However, it is not necessary to depend en-

tirely on the government for that, and we should not
want to do so.

But beyond any conceivable improvement of
what economists know, we must look for better
economic policy to a more far-sighted attitude by the
government's policy makers. And that in turn will
depend on the attitude of the public. Surely it should
come as no surprise to be told that in a democracy the
quality of public policy will depend on the quality of
public attitudes.

There has been some evidence in the last year or
so that the public has learned an important lesson in
the decade of inflation. It is less insistent on ex-
pansive monetary and fiscal policy than it would
once have been in the face of the unemployment we
have been experiencing. Also, there seems to be less
faith in price and wage controls as a solution for our
problems than there once was.

This advance in public understanding is en-
couraging for the future performance of our
economy. Whether the advance comes fast enough,
and how to accelerate it, are serious questions. It is to
this area, and not to the devising of paper programs
for national economic planning, that our attention
needs to be devoted.

DISCUSSANT

Israel M. Kirzner *

*Professor of Economics, New York University

Some time ago, Paul Samuelson recalled a great debate that took place at Harvard many years earlier. The debate was between two formidable opponents, Joseph Schumpeter on the one hand, and the Marxist Paul Sweezy on the other; the topic was "The Future of Capitalism." In the chair was one of today's very distinguished lecturers, Professor Wassily Leontief. "Great debaters," Samuelson observed, "deserve great moderators," and that night Leontief was in fine form. At the end he fairly summarized the viewpoints expressed:

The patient is capitalism. What is to be his fate? Our speakers are in fact agreed that the patient is inevitably dying. But the bases of their diagnoses could not be more different.
On the one hand there is Sweezy, who utilizes the analysis of Marx and Lenin to deduce that

the patient is dying of a malignant cancer. Absolutely no operation can help. The end is foreordained.

On the other hand, there is Schumpeter. He, too, and rather cheerfully, admits that the patient is dying.... But to Schumpeter, the patient is dying of a psychosomatic ailment. Not cancer but neurosis is his complaint. Filled with self-hate, he has lost the will to live. [1]

We have again had the very same patient— *mirabile dictu* still alive—on the examining table (if not on the psychiatrist's couch). And, once again, two eminent doctors, this time Professor Leontief himself being one of them, have differed in their diagnoses. Both authorities are dissatisfied with the patient's overall condition. Their anxious attention has focussed on the patient's heart, the market. Dr. Stein has given us, on the whole, a reassuring report. The market, he finds, is a basically healthy organ. The patient's somewhat erratic performance in recent years must be attributed, not to cardiac-related problems, but to gaps in our economic knowledge, reinforced by unwise public opinions. Tampering with the patient's heart through the introduction of planning, Dr. Stein warns, is highly dangerous. Alleviation of the patient's condition is to be looked for in an array of considerably milder prescriptions

[1] P. A. Samuelson, *The Samuelson Sampler* (Glen Ridge: T. Horton and Co., 1973), p. 261.

including a regimen of intensified economic research, expanded collection of statistics, and a wiser public.

Dr. Leontief, in contrast, finds the patient's condition far more serious and calling for much bolder and more imaginative treatment. The patient's heart, Dr. Leontief regretfully discovers, suffers from grave congenital defects which inevitably manifest themselves in resource misallocation, spasms of unemployment, and idle capacity. Drastic open-heart surgery is called for, Dr. Leontief believes, which will subordinate the fitful operation of the market to carefully designed and computerized planning procedures. This treatment, it is believed, while it will indeed drastically alter the aged inner works of the system, can get the patient back on his feet behaving in a manner which his old business friends will find reassuringly familiar. If these businessmen really love this patient, we infer, they will delay not one Congressional session longer, and will support immediate surgery regardless of the financial or ideological sacrifices called for.

From this clash of opinion among the experts there emerges clear agreement on one crucial point, namely, that the debate over national economic planning hinges on the ability of the market system, the profit system, the free enterprise system, to deliver the goods, and, in particular, on the degree to which a national economic planning system (with or without a coercive machinery for its implementation) can emulate or surpass the performance of the free market. This is, as Professor Stein has made clear, by no means a new question. But the lectures do provide scope for some critical observations.

Two small details in Professor Leontief's remarks are especially noteworthy. The first of these
consists in his careful explanation that national
economic planning will provide to citizens a series of
alternative detailed *feasible* plans from among which
they can then choose. Professor Leontief does not
claim that any of these feasible plans, among all *conceivable* national patterns of production, is in any
sense an *optimal* one. After all, a set of alternative
plans, based as they must be on past input-output
structural patterns, may simply fail to include equally
feasible possibilities which, in the light of current
tastes and technological knowledge, might easily be
judged as in some sense better than those on the planners' menu of options.

The second detail to be noted arises out of yet
another of Professor Leontief's delightfully apt
metaphors. In discussing how planners can harness
the force of the profit motive towards the implementation of their plan, Leontief likens their task to that
of the hydraulic engineer charged with regulating a
major water system. In his work the engineer must
take full advantage of the force of gravity, but must
plan dams, dikes, and locks in such a manner as to
take advantage of gravity without permitting it to
create floods or devastating droughts. For Leontif
the profit motive, the driving force in the market
system, is like gravity both in its potential for good if
controlled; and its potential for disaster if left un-
controlled.

A similarly powerful metaphor has been used
elsewhere by Professor Leontief which confirms this

perception by him of the market process.[2] In that
metaphor the economy is seen as a sailing ship propelled by a powerful wind, the profit motive. But to
permit the vessel, we are warned, simply to go before
the wind without use of the rudder, is to ensure that
the ship will veer off its course and land on the rocks.

Both of these rich metaphors clearly present
Professor Leontief's appreciation of the market as a
force which carries with it no assurance whatever that
the direction towards which, without guidance, it
tends is a desirable one rather than a catastrophic
one. Now this view surely calls for comment. To be
sure any defense of the market must recognize and
come to grips with a number of well-known possible
problems in its operation. But to see the entrepreneurial profit motive as a force as likely to
result in harm as in benefit, cannot but cause surprise.

The crux of the matter is that every opportunity
for entrepreneurial profit arises from the existence of
two market prices for essentially the same product or
the same bundle of inputs. This price divergence,
which offers the opportunity for profit is, therefore,
at the same time, evidence of an earlier failure of
coordination among members or sectors of the
economy. The drive to capture profits is, then, a
drive to locate pockets of inefficiency. The successful
capture of pure entrepreneurial profits occurs only
through action which tends to eliminate the price

[2]W. Leontief, "Sails and Rudders, Ship of State," in L. Silk
(ed.), *Capitalism the Moving Target* (New York, Praeger, 1974).

spread and the inefficiency which was its cause. The ceaseless agitation of the market is thus not propelled by an undirected force, but by an extraordinarily sensitive detector of gaps in coordination. This agitation consists, therefore, in a continuing tendency to coordinate economic activity in the face of ceaseless changes in consumer preferences, resource availabilities, and technological knowledge.

In thus sniffing out existing failures of coordination, therefore, the market achieves more than merely a tendency towards the attainment of a set of mutually feasible activities. It tends towards *optimality*. But optimality is something which, as Professor Stein has suggested, and as Professor Leontief has, if I understand him correctly, not denied, national economic planning is unable to claim.

The distinction between feasibility and optimality is so important, and so instructive for an understanding of the limitations of national planning, that I venture a small parable of my own as an illustration of that distinction.

Imagine someone wishing to buy exactly thirty dollars worth of groceries at the local supermarket, who happens to be rather weak in arithmetic, and is quite intimidated by the tens of thousands of variously priced items on the shelves. The shopper is well aware that there are many millions of ways in which to spend his thirty dollars. If an expert offers to provide a list of half a dozen arithmetically airtight ways of spending thirty dollars, based on records of how this same shopper and other shoppers spent their grocery budgets in the past, our shopper is surely entitled to be doubtful. Our shopper may well feel that, while each of these alternative buying proposals is *feasible* in the sense that it requires no more than thirty dollars and leaves no money unspent none of them is likely to be *optimal*. There is no assurance that any of these proposals has taken into account the shopper's own changes in tastes since last week, or the supermarket's changes in offerings, or even the likelihood that last week's purchases were themselves suboptimal. The shopper may well feel that a better market basket—even if one arithmetically less than perfect—might result from a keen, curious, and enterprising *personal* exploration of the supermarket corridors.

Both of our distinguished lecturers have referred to widespread dissatisfaction with the performance of contemporary capitalism. It is this dissatisfaction which underlies the call for national economic planning, to supplement or supplant sole reliance on a faltering market system. Our perception of what it is that the free market tends to achieve suggests, surely, an alternative and superior path along which to search for improvements.

Professor Stein has referred to the past forty years as decades during which we have formed the broad consensus that we should assign the principal economic role to the free market, and confine the role of the government to the task of maintaining a stable and competitive framework within which the market might operate. We need not necessarily dispute this reading of the dominant view of things during the past four decades. But it must surely be pointed out that, in its rather uninhibited interpretation of the assigned role of the state, the dominant view has, during this very same period, permitted and encouraged an unprecedented explosion in the volume of governmental activity, manifesting itself in an enormous growth in the size of government itself, in a volume of regulation and intervention which has seriously constricted and distorted the scope for the competitive market process, and, above all, in an inflation of the money supply which has introduced profound and potentially catastrophic distortions all of its own.

May it not just be possible that what our sluggish and fitful patient needs for recovery, is not a heart-transplant, nor even a crash program of economic research and expanded gathering of statistics but simply fresh air, sunshine, good food and exercise, free of the addictive drug of monetary inflation, of the crushing weight of a bloated public sector, and of the mass of regulations which hamper the flow of the spontaneous and invigorating juices of free competition?

DISCUSSANT

John R. Stark*

*Executive Director, Joint Economic Committee, United States Congress

At the outset, let me say that Professor Stein has done us a favor by pointing out the variety of meanings that the word "planning" holds for different people.

There is a tendency to see the debate in terms of strict polarity—pro and con. Either you are for a government dictatorship or you favor rule of the robber barons.

The semicircle would be a more appropriate analogy. We are all positioned on an arc looking toward that golden city in the distance. And I suppose that the mecca that we seek is an economy of high employment, efficient resource utilization, growth, stability, and an equitable income distribution. (One that is consonant with a democratic society.)

In seeking this common ground, I suggest that we basically agree, first, on the great need for improved coordination of the public sector, and second, the requirement that it be done within the framework of a free democratic system.

As someone involved in economic policy making in the Congress, I would like to make some observations from my own point on that point of the circle. At the present time, government domination has become one of the devils in our national election year morality play. Therefore, it might be helpful to develop some useful standards for assessing the strength of this demon. Two tests of the relative health and freedom of the private sector, are the ownership of property and control of the income derived from such property. Virtually all of our system of production, that is, our income producing assets, are privately owned. The Federal share is about 2 percent. There are of course limitations on the use of property in every society. These limitations are growing in modern economies because economic life is becoming more complex and interdependent. Availability of raw materials, energy, food, population, environment; all of these have to be considered and usually involve public action. Likewise, the income from property is affected by government regulation of various kinds, for example, taxes, minimum wages, and environmental safeguards.

There is a basic question which is both practical and philosophical as to the point at which inhibition on the private use of income may become inconsistent with a democratic society. But I see nothing in any present discussion of planning in the Congress that materially changes the perspective on that score. Let me be more specific. The Federal

Government already maintains an extensive and complex, though poorly coordinated, involvement in the economy. Consider: Over 25 percent of the national income passes through Federal hands, coming in as taxes and going out as expenditures. Beyond that, the government maintains a number of regulatory functions that affect, in a very fundamental way, important sections of the economy, such as transportation, communication, ocean shipping, financial markets, and a variety of others. The Federal Government plays a role as investor, as in the case of the space industry, which was financed entirely from Federal funds. This program has had extensive ramifications for the economy. The Federal Government builds facilities on a substantial scale. Our Federal investment in interstate highways alone, in the past twenty years, has exceeded $100 billion, with pervasive consequences for our economic development. The Federal Government exercises a strong effect on credit markets. It is a large borrower. It lends directly for many purposes. It guarantees loans.

The fact that this massive involvement lacks direction and coordination gives it a capricious quality that makes the burden more onerous for private enterprise. Last summer, Gunnar Myrdal told me that, you have Government controls of all sorts over your private lives and still you are proud of having no planning. If you had more planning for the big things in society, then you would not have to interfere so much with individual activity.

We all know that there is an extensive network of influence and self-interest that is constantly brought to bear on the formulation of public policy. To put it bluntly, when good government coordination and direction are missing, the strong elements in the society become more assertive just as the medieval barons were strong when the king was weak. Washington is full of lobbyists. Their job is to see that the web of Federal involvement is as comfortable as possible for them and their clients. As an example, recent energy programs emanating from The White House and the Congress reflect the proportionate strengths of organized groups in each of these branches.

Admittedly, the United States today lacks sufficient capability to organize any kind of complete planning competence, on an instantaneous basis. We must develop it. It will be slow. But I am not pessimistic. I recall as a member of the armed forces in World War II how inadequately we were prepared when we first entered the war. Indeed, the German High Command was of the opinion we could not survive a long war. So I think many of the fears that planning programs will founder on government incompetence are wrong. The same was said about the Employment Act when it was considered in 1944 and 1945. It was also said about the Budget Act which was passed in 1974 and many others. Also, in the past eight years, we have seen an unusual confrontation between the Executive Branch and the Congress. This has tended to frustrate constructive initiatives and vitiate healthy functioning of government. Also, the Administration's ideological bias against policies that involve any kind of intervention in the economy has added to the negative ambience.

Doctor Stein has stressed the vagueness of the goals of the Humphrey-Javits Bill. That may be true. I might add that we in the United States have shown a general tendency to be vague in our national efforts to formulate policy goals. We tend to combine means and ends; for example, we want better allocation of resources, improved education, fuller employment, and justice for all.

Right now there is a good deal of effort going into a Full Employment Bill. Inevitably, it will have to be related to planning proposals. If we are to improve our employment performance, then obviously a more involved policy programming is required. The continued emphasis on the employment legislation seems to indicate that most politicians are more comfortable with an effort pointed more precisely toward a general objective, namely, employment.

Of course, there is a substantial amount of planning that now goes on regularly, both in the government and in industry. Unfortunately, it is not coordinated. The Congress is constantly bombarded by recommendations from government departments and trade groups proposing long-range policies with pervasive economic effects. Most of these necessarily are based on some assumption or other as to the prospective development of the economy, the outlook, emergency needs, prices, and wages. Almost always these assumptions are inarticulate; most of the time, they are poorly founded. They are a mixture of presumption and knowledge, sometimes insight, but, all too often, self-interest.

The substantial amount of private industry planning that goes on in our economy has to be done under present conditions without reference to related plans in other industries and the government even though there is an inevitable interdependence. Professor Leontief recognizes the value of consensus planning to such efforts.

At the International Economic Conference in Stockholm, Sweden, the point was made that a lack of a policy consensus in an advanced economy tends to increase inflation. If there is not any kind of clarity about policy prospects, groups with market power tend to protect themselves by trying to grab a larger share of the national income. This is significant.

At the same time, we must recognize, as Doctor Stein and others have pointed out, the difficulty of obtaining a consensus as to long range economic prospects for the economy. It will take time and effort. But I think we must make the effort, and, in any case, it will be better than the confusion that now prevails.

Just consider the extensive network of tax inducements and subsidies contained in our Federal budget. These were all enacted on the basis of some assumption or other as to the need for affecting resource allocation through public action. As I said, the assumptions were often wrong or misguided and the efforts quite different from original expectations.

I found it disturbing to see this extensive and constant public intervention in the economy, while there is no effort to develop articulated targets of general consensus. Because of the dominant role of the public sector in the economy, I doubt we can afford this any more.

Increasingly, those of us engaged in policy making in Federal, private, country, state, and local sectors see a growing need for some kind of consensus as to our future economic development. Professor Leontief makes this point very persuasively in my opinion.

From my own experience, I have concluded that policy makers in both the private sector and public sector are not willing to rely solely on the price system to bring about necessary adjustments in investment, credit, and production of basic materials. The growth of public involvement will continue whether we like it or not. Inevitably, this will involve more and more interrelation between public and private policy makers in seeking mutual agreement on long-range objectives. It is going on and I think it will lead soon to more explicit national planning. I mean this in the sense not of coercion, but of consensus. We will decide on objectives, determine resource availability and influence investment patterns. Already, public involvement is producing a more detailed and continuing relation between public and private policy makers in certain sectors of the economy. Radical chic of today, may be the Sears Roebuck of tomorrow.

The real question is one of control of the process. Will it be done by an elite body of insiders, either a corporacy or a labor elite or a combination of both, or do we try to handle it in the framework of our Democratic society? Like E. M. Forster I say "Two cheers for Democracy."

APPENDIX

APPENDIX I
THE CASE FOR AND AGAINST
NATIONAL ECONOMIC PLANNING*

John Kenneth Galbraith
Henry Wallich
Melville J. Ulmer
Murray L. Weidenbaum

Reprinted by Permission of Challenge

JOHN KENNETH GALBRAITH: I'm not going to make a case for planning, because this is an audience of high intelligence, great liberality of mind, deep percipience. You already know that planning is something within the governmental apparatus of the United States that we already do—that is already required in response both to circumstances and to institutional change. So the case is only for doing it better, more consciously, and I think this is of considerable importance, with terminological clarity. I believe we should call planning, planning.

Let us consider the scale of such planning activities in the government of the United States at the present time. The most obvious case is, of course, the Council of Economic Advisers which makes macroeconomic projections, and indicates the policies appropriate to those projections. The Council has clear jurisdiction, at least, as regards advice, in fiscal and

monetary policy. As Professor Lindbeck said last
night in his excellent address, the process of modern
macroeconomic management is a complicated
multisector enterprise in which, among other things,
problems of wages and incomes policy arise. I expect
that the Council of Economic Advisers is now very
much concerned as it looks at the wage negotiations
for 1976 and the effect also of a possibly stronger
labor market. This is a jurisdiction which it also
shares with the Department of Labor. In the past
week or two, we have observed some of the planning
in that Department, this being the concessions won
from the unions in connection with the lamented
common-situs picketing bill.

    We see also much planning in a field with which
I was once closely familiar—that of agriculture.
There was a time in the distant past when Earl Butz
was considered to be the leader of the retarded wing
of the agricultural economics profession, and I was
associated with the progressive wing. In those respec-
tive positions, we developed a certain respect for each
other. Although he remains with the retarded wing,
Earl has recently been engaged in rather forthright
long-term planning in relation to agricultural ex-
ports. This is in a part of the economy where even
those of us who have doubts about the continued
power of market forces concede that they still have a
substantial role.

    It's commonplace that during this past year
we've had a great deal of planning in the field of
energy resources and conservation. And indeed
legislation implementing such planning is only a few
days old. Here the need is widely recognized by an

avowedly conservative Administration. What distinguishes the Administration in this field is reluctance. Its reference is not to a planner, but to a czar, most possibly because a czar is considered more democratic than a planner. Or it could be because nobody has told Republicans what comes after czars.

I could go on to cite the very large area of planning having to do with environmental effects. I would urge that in a world where a very large part of the economy is preempted by oligopolies, where prices are administered—points on which few will think that Galbraith is on novel ground—there is no reliable equilibrating influence deriving from the market. This is combined with the further circumstances of a heavy dependence for supplies on countries—socialist or nonsocialist—that do not avow any commitment to the market. But at home there can be no pretense that the development of the supply of electrical energy in New York City will be related by the market to the demand for air-conditioned buildings. Problems arise here which as a matter of simple prudence should be perceived, must be foreseen. This is a most important area of planning.

I think if I were bold enough I would even go on to cite some other institutions which have some concern for the future and which do not retreat to the market. I would, for example, fold the Federal Reserve System into this complex of planning institutions were Governor Wallich not here. However, he is in a position to deny out of firsthand knowledge that the Federal Reserve does any planning of any sort, thus brutally undermining my position.

So I urge passage of the legislation now before
Congress. It makes conscious our efforts in this pro-
ces; it causes us to recognize that planning must be
in some degree planned.

I would make only one other point. It would be
of advantage not only to society but also to our profession, were this legislation to cause the Council of
Economic Advisers to disappear. There is a life cycle
for economic or official bodies; they're better in their
youth than they are in their senility. The Council of
Economic Advisers has run the course of that cycle
and we would do well to see it become part of this
larger planning process. The notion of a three-man
board of detached advisers, in touch with ultimate
wisdom, ultimate science, ultimate truth, is
something we are now rather too sophisticated to
take seriously. As the Council has become increasingly politicized, it has become something of an embar-
rassment to the economics profession. Its forecasts
no longer have much relation to what anyone expects
to happen. They reflect an almost 100 percent cor-
relation with what a particular administration needs
to have happen. Yet its statements are solemnly
labeled economic forecasts; they're presented to the
public as the best work of our profession. They are a
fraud which anyone with any regard for the profes-
sional reputation of economists should be rather concerned about.

HENRY WALLICH: I came here with two expectations. One was that Ken Galbraith would make a
good defense of the existing system; and by my
reading, that expectation hasn't been altogether

wrong. My second expectation was that if a prize were to be awarded for a new argument for or against planning, this prize would probably remain un-awarded tonight. Whether I was right on that or not still remains to be seen.

Obviously everybody plans, every government plans. Planning seems to be simply a question of common sense. To go beyond this conclusion, and also beyond the theoretical pros and cons of plan-ning, one would have to look at specific planning ex-periences. That's what I propose to do by drawing upon the planning experience of Germany and Japan in the postwar period.

Let's take the Japanese economy after World War II. The Japanese economy has been one of the most successful in the postwar period with its GNP doubling in ten years or less. Now Japan can be regarded as a country where public planning plays a very considerable role.

The political context of the Japanese orientation toward public planning is important. Students of the Japanese way of life refer to Japan as a consent society. That is to say, the predominant mode of group decision-making is through consensus rather than confrontation or competition. They make a great effort to avoid overruling or outvoting anybody. You can imagine that the process is often slow, conveying to the outsider an impression of hesitancy and indecision. But once everybody has signed off on a decision, you can count on action that is general and forceful.

The environment in which Japan found itself after World War II has favored effective planning

for rapid growth. I suppose that, even if market
forces had been allowed to hold sway unmitigated by
public planning, Japan would have found itself moving rapidly in the direction of big industrial power
status. What the Japanese did was to accelerate considerably this nearly inevitable trend. This tendency
to plan along the grain of market forces, rather than
against it, seems to have been characteristic of
Japan's public policy. All this tells me that the
Japanese technique of group decision-making, plus
the economic opportunities which Japan en-
countered, helped to make economic planning effective.

Take another country that was successful after
World War II—Germany. Now the Germans, being
orderly and systematic, could hardly help planning.
But to a large degree, the German backed away very
deliberately from a tightly planned economy after the
war and opted for a market-oriented economy. The
Germans explained their preference for the market
specifically on the grounds of the favorable performance characteristics of the market system. The
results achieved, as we know, do not contradict that
view.

So the historical evidence, it seems to me, is that
different countries have done very well in different
ways. We can conclude only that there must be
something in the circumstances of each particular
country that explains differences in procedures and
results.

Now let's turn to the United States. Our political
process—and I think to some extent this encompasses
every form of public and private organization—is

one of competition and confrontation. It is a familiar dictum that politics is the art of compromise. But compromise often takes place only after a bruising battle in which somebody assembles a majority, perhaps no more than 51 percent of the vote. The winner takes all; the loser's consent is not solicited—very much in contrast to Japanese practice. It is a procedure that seems to have worked well for us, but I must confess that this process would seem to make effective planning difficult. It seems to me that market processes have been appropriate to the American environment. The market avoids confrontation by utilizing anonymous decision-making by the consumer to decide what is to be produced. The market processes of profit and utility maximization reconcile competing objectives without severe political conflicts.

Let's look at our situation today. Now, thanks to the appearance of Ken's *The Affluent Society* in 1958, we know that it is not production that is lacking in this country. We're producing enough, so we would not be planning for production as the Japanese have done.

Planning in the U.S., I suspect, would be principally for use. Planning for use, combined with our process of confrontation, suggests that extreme promises may have to be made to assemble a majority. The likely consequence of these excessive promises, it seems to me, would be a continuing condition of excess demand. Excess demand leads to inflation; inflation may in turn lead to price and wage controls. I am not happy with what I see at the end of that road called national planning.

In short, what I observe is that there are countries like Japan where it may be possible, indeed it *is* possible to plan effectively without creating social dissent and unrealistic expectations. There are countries where it might be possible to plan effectively, as in Germany, where for political and economic reasons, a decision has been made not to engage in systematic national planning. There are countries like our own which are debating whether we should plan more.

I think we ought to ask ourselves: Does our way of doing things lend itself to this process? I've given you two reasons for thinking that our strength does not lie in this direction: I suspect that planning would lead to divisive political confrontation, and I think that planning would lead to excessive demands upon the economy.

Finally, planning in the United States, given our habits, would probably lead to an underestimate of the need for production and an overestimate of what can be and should be consumed. This follows from the role that you see the producer playing in American society. If it's true, as Ken said years ago, that we have solved the problems of production, then it follows naturally that the concerns of the nonproducer outrank those of the producer. The young, the old, the unemployed, the welfare recipients— these are all people who deserve our attention, but they are all nonproducers. The producer pays. I suspect that planning under these conditions would allocate too little to investment, too much to consumption. We would find ourselves in the end with slower growth and fewer resources than we would

have had, if we had relied on the free market instead
of planning.

Again, in support of this analysis, look at the
frequency with which our main public objectives
have shifted over the last fifteen years. We have worried at times about inflation, at times about the environment or energy independence; we've worried
about problems of welfare; we've worried—and I
think rightly—about a series of shifting concerns
partly economic, partly noneconomic. In other
words, we have been ready to change our national
goals very rapidly.

I think that if you are to have an efficient and effective planning process, you would have to have
greater steadiness in national objectives than we have
so far shown. If we want to treat ourselves to the luxury of rapidly changing objectives, as we might well
be justified in doing, then we'd better not reach too
deeply into the economy and try to predetermine the
course of events. Planning and the lengthy process of
installing the corresponding technology are likely to
freeze the structure of production. With our short
public attention span, we are likely to find ourselves
dissatisfied with our economy and its objectives. To
make matters worse, planning, as opposed to more
flexible private decision-making processes in
response to rapidly shifting goals, will produce
disorder and waste.

Well, let me conclude. National economic planning in the United States seems to me to propose the
wrong thing in the wrong country at the wrong time.
Given the American way of making group decisions,
given our excessive emphasis on short-run objectives

that shift frequently, and given the unsympathetic treatment meted out to the producer, I see little good coming from intensified public planning.

MELVILLE J. ULMER: We economists take no little pride, I think, in formulating models in relative rather than in absolute terms, always with an eagle eye out for the alternatives open in problems of choice. For example, more sensitively than most, we perceive that growing òld is a good, a *normal* good that is, over most of its range, because of the comparative advantage it holds over the only possible alternative. Now I think it helps considerably to view national planning in the same light. That is, we need to judge it, like other things, in relation to its alternatives, and understand thereby its comparative advantages. Practically, there is only one alternative I know of, and that is more or less what we have in the United States today which, as I see it, is a situation of unplanned, or displanned intervention in nearly every branch of economic life. True, theoretically laissez-faire is a third alternative, but that position overlooks entirely the history of how we got into the situation we're in now. I refer not to the quality of specific measures of the state today, but to the reason for their existence. Do they represent, at least in part, a response to real, serious and possibly solvable problems? With the exception of the lunatic fringe of libertarians, everyone, I think, recognizes today that pollution, environmental destruction, waste, industrial injuries, poverty, unemployment, inflation and so on are real problems, and that, however ineffectually, government has responded to them. So the

question, why plan, boils down in practice to a choice
between the status quo, more or less, and some other
approach to the economic role of government. That
government must have a significant economic role, it
seems to me, is beyond question, unless we attribute
to it all of our ills, including pollution, and contamination of food and drugs.

A recent meeting on this subject, at which I was
an observer, was called by a committee of philan-
thropic educators, drawn from the upper end of *For-
tune*'s 500 largest corporations. They described planning this way: an economic planning board is born,
the members of which all bear a remarkable
resemblance to Josef Stalin. The board inserts its
quantified goals of final national output into a linear
programming model of the American economy. Professor Leontif, who fortunately bears a Russian
name, provides the underlying input-output coeffi-
cients. A few adjustments, corrections, manipula-
tions, the computer spins again and the planning
board reads off the optimum price and quantity for
every good and service in the American economy.
Enter the master of imperative planning, whose duty
it is to impose these results on the American people.
He appears, in their picture, in the strikingly tall,
slender figure of a Canadian-American who once
taught at Harvard. I've exaggerated only slightly.

Extraordinarily frenetic though that portrait
may be, it contains two common misconceptions that
need to be confronted. First of all, there's nothing
more authoritarian about economic regulations, in a
democracy, than there is about traffic laws. Like the
traffic laws, they're to be judged exclusively by their

results. Secondly, to discover what in fact planning
would do, we've got to steer clear of wearily con-
cocted fantasies and hark back to those basic
economic problems, pragmatically drawn from experience, to which government has already
responded for good or ill—and to which planning, as
the first order of business, would also have to respond. Can planning make a substantive and
valuable difference? That's the question.

One difference lies in a contrast in institutional
outlook. At present, government in America operates
on the fundamental premise that the market, the free
market, can do no wrong—in general, that is. Hence
government is thrust into an unchanging posture of
constant surprise. We are suprised that inflation occurs and accelerates every time business activity is ex-
panding, even though it has been doing so repeatedly
for 30 years. We are even more surprised when inflation doesn't disappear as corrective recessions are in-
voked, even though prices have risen every year but
one since World War II; and we're surprised about
pollution and poverty, food and drug contamination,
urban squalor, crime in inner cities and so on, even
though all are equally predictable, and without the
aid of econometric models. Surprise makes for hectic
ineffectuality in government—the waste and proliferation of agencies, often operating at cross purposes, that Murray Weidenbaum has so aptly
described and may possibly expand upon this after-
noon.

In contrast, economic planning requires a
pragmatic governmental attitude of readiness, the
same alertness and forethought that any sensible per-

son exercises in his own affairs. At a minimum, it would result in the coordination of what government is trying to do now, in its displanned, disorganized way. The organization of a planning board, unless democratic processes collapsed entirely, would be obligated to see to that. But that's simply a minimum. Beyond that, we'd undoubtedly have a much more active government than we have now. I don't mean necessarily a larger government. Much of what we do at present is wasted or perverted by special interests. Yet planning would mean a truly busier government, simply because so many public needs now go unattended. On this matter, no doubt, the issues raised require more than the ten minutes allotted to me, which are now fading. But the basic question is this: are there serious problems of society today whose solution demands a more positive response from government than we could possibly get without a planning mechanism?

I think full employment without inflation is one of these. It is insoluble now, and yet its achievement would be manageable under planning. But so would offsets to the present antisocial behavior of oligopolistic industry, in all its manifestations; the narrowly aggressive behavior of unions; the multiple market failures and externalities that increasingly crowd the textbooks; and some that are not mentioned. These, like the so-called energy crisis, suggest the empirical questions which would induce us to compare what we have now, what we are likely to get under present circumstances, and what we could possibly achieve by other means.

Fundamentally, in many aspects of public

policy, planning means freedom from dead ideologies, as it certainly does in problems of economic stability. And it means, especially, freedom to use the power of government to subordinate all the other desiderata of society, like profits or growth, to the central one of furthering the public interest.

MURRAY WEIDENBAUM: I want to start off by accentuating the positive. Let me do that by attempting to add a moral or religious dimension to the discussion of planning. At this point I wish to invoke the memory of the patron saint of planning. I am referring, of course, to Robert Burns, and especially to his immortal line about "the best-laid plans." And my formal remarks will indeed be in that spirit. I will focus on one specific aspect of the debate on a formal national economic planning system in the United States. Let's not trip over those words lightly; we're not talking about the Treasury planning to buy enough paper to print enough income tax returns for us to fill out by April 15. We're talking about a formal national economic planning system.

The one aspect I wish to cover is the supposed parallel between business planning and government planning. I think analyzing that is very instructive. I wish to recall that key proponents of the proposed national economic planning system, including both Senator Humphrey and Senator Javits, contend that since planning is acceptable for business—well, it ought to be equally acceptable for government. That is such a simple proposition that it seems self-evident.

Yet those of us who have been involved in decision-making in both the public and the private sectors are keenly aware of the important differences between public and private planning. As a former planner in the aerospace industry—volunarily retired, I should add—I can recall that for a number of years industry looked to Lockheed for the most sophisticated and widely emulated long-range planning. You may recall the slogan, "Look to Lockheed for leadership." Lockheed? We may wonder if business planning is a case of the closer you get, the worse it looks. I want to report a little research on that very question. How successful has business planning been? Then I'll draw a few parallels.

First of all, we must acknowledge, there are no objective measurements in the literature. We do, however, have a variety of evaluations by informed observers. And they all come to virtually the same conclusions. I'll quote just a few. David Ewing, in his classic study of business planning, tells us, "The paradox is that the planning movement, despite such strong motives to make it succeed, has not generally been blessed with success. The triumphs have been stunning—but few." E. Kirby Warren, in another key study, concludes that few executives are satisfied with their company's ability to translate planning into meaningful practice. It's intriguing to note that he found that each company he studied took solace in the fact that while it was not doing a very good job in planning, neither were any of its competitors. Robert J. Mockler, looking at the state of the art of planning said, "In spite of the advances made during the

1960s, relatively few companies have developed effective planning operations—although many have
tried."

And certainly many business firms in the United
States do continue to engage in formal long-range
planning. I think it's instructive to understand their
motives; they do give a variety of reasons, not all of
which may comfortably fit the rationale for government planning. Some managements always state that
planning is a powerful instrument for tightening
organizational discipline and control. Others maintain that planning can be used to lend authenticity to
the corporate leader. A chief executive with a formal
plan, neatly printed and illustrated, provides the im-
age of having the management task well in hand. I
don't find this terribly compelling as a guide to
public policy.

But more important are the fundamental differences between business and government planning.
Essentially we're viewing the difference between
forecasting and reacting to the future, on the one
hand, in the private sector; and trying to control it,
on the other, in the public sector. Corporate planning
is based of necessity on the attempt to persuade the
rest of society that they ought to purchase the goods
and services produced by a given firm. The controls
that may accompany a plan are internally oriented.
n striking contrast, the government is sovereign. Its
planning ultimately involves coercion, the use of its
power to achieve the results it desires. Its controls are
externally oriented, extending to the society at large.
The proponents of a formal national planning
system—and here I'm delighted to quote scripture, if

you will, that is, the articles in *Challenge* by the Initiative Committee for National Economic Planning—state that they do not want to set specific goals for General Motors, for General Electric or for any other firm. But what would they do if these companies did not conduct themselves in the aggregate in accordance with the national plan? Would they leave the actual results to chance? Or to the free market? Hardly. The Initiative Committee states that the planning office "would try to induce the relevant industries to act accordingly." And the inducements are not trivial. The government's power to tax, to purchase, to subsidize, to assist and to regulate are awesome. The most powerful planning system in the private sector lacks the ability to levy taxes.

Much of the rhetoric favored in the national economic planning system is in terms of developing better information—surely a worthy objective. But even a cursory examination of the literature on business planning demonstrates that planning is intended to be far more than improved information gathering. Robert G. Murdick offers a basic definition. What are we talking about when we say planning? "A plan is a predetermined course of action...to accomplish a specific set of objectives." Ewing offers the most terse rendition: "Planning is to a large extent the job of making things happen that would not otherwise occur."

The proponents of centralized government planning do not leave the matter in a vacuum, and I quote the Initiative Committee: "The heart of planning is to go from information to action." I believe that the essence of the difference between public and private

planning is the locus of the decision-making. If Ford
or GM are not selling as many autos as they had
planned, there are a limited number of things they
can do. Within their available resources, they can
lower prices, or change the nature of the product—
but look at the demise of the Edsel, the LaSalle, the
DeSoto. Often they're simply forced to abandon the
project. The consumer, the maligned consumer, remains the ultimate decision-maker.

The situation is far different in the public sector.
If the government does not believe the American
public is buying enough cars,it can lower the price as
much as it likes by a tax deduction. It can subsidize a
private manufacturer or simply take over the ownership of the auto industry. Let me quote Senator
Hubert Humphrey, the co-author of the bill. He
makes the point far more colorfully. "What can
government do about it? Government can do a lot
about it. For example, the size of automobiles...can
be influenced a great deal by taxing cubic displace-
ment, horsepower or weight....Government can also
influence industry by giving an investment tax credit
to companies that produce fuel-efficient
automobiles. These are just two ways in which
government policy can influence the private
economy." Humphrey goes on to point out that
government is a large purchaser of goods and services. And again I quote, "Everybody else fades into
insignificance in comparison. From the viewpoint of
purchasing power, General Motors is a peanut stand
compared to the United States Government." I
couldn't have said it any better.

My point is not that private planning does not

involve control but that those subject to its control are very different. Once a private corporation adopts its long-range plan it may push damn hard on the various units of the company to meet those goals and objectives, but the incentives and sanctions are focused on the officers, the employees of the company. If things go wrong, the onus falls on them. Government planning, in contrast, focuses on guiding or influencing, and thus ultimately controlling the activities of the entire nation. If things go wrong in public sector planning, it will be the taxpayer and consumer who bear the hurt.

I do think it's important to distinguish two types of government planning. I don't mean good and bad, although that may be useful too. I mean external planning, which is what I've been discussing, and which involves all sorts of extensions of government power over the private sector, as opposed to internal planning, which may be more comparable to private planning. Internal government planning relates to management of the government's own activities. Again, let me quote my second favorite economist from Minnesota, Hubert Humphrey: "We don't have any economic impact statement for governmental decisions. The government goes around willy-nilly making decisions of consequence. There was no estimate of the economic impact of the Occupational Safety Act.... I happen to be for the occupational safety program, but what were its economic implications? Did anyone think that through? No.... The manner in which we are presently utilizing government resources and government agencies is a haphazard, helter-skelter enterprise."

Ladies and gentlemen, I would suspect that if government is being conducted on such a haphazard, helter-skelter basis, it would be rather reluctant to take on the extremely ambitious task of managing the entire economy. Incidentally, we don't have to guess what the results would be of applying business planning techniques to government. They did try, but without exactly inspiring confidence. To those of you who are rusty on ancient American history, let us recall that in August 1965, President Lyndon Johnson announced with great fanfare the introduction of what he called a "very new and very revolutionary system of planning and programming and budgeting throughout the vast federal government, so that through the tools of modern management, the full promise of a finer life can be brought to every American at the lowest possible cost." I'm referring to what we call in the trade "PPBS." And those initials, I think, were very potently selected. In retrospect, it's clear that PPBS did not help the federal government avoid fundamental overcommitments either at home or abroad. In fact it's intriguing that some of the same people—the same person who was involved in the failure of the Edsel in the private sector—were instrumental in introducing PPBS, etc., into the public sector. And they are also resposnsible for some of the major achievements during that period, the deeper American involvement in the Vietnam War, the overpromising of the Great Society programs. Now my point is a modest one. It's not that the attempt back then to introduce organized planning led to those failures, but simply that it clearly did not prevent them.

Perhaps we should be pleased that the results were mainly paper-shuffling, wheel-spinning exercises. In a fine article in *Challenge* (March/April, 1975), John Sheahan analyzed French planning and pointed out what I think should be an important caution—the possibility that large corporations would dominate the government planning process. As an aside, this would be an extension of the widely held "capture" theory of federal regulatory agencies, whereby we believe that often the industries being regulated come to dominate the decisions of the agencies set up to regulate them. Sheahan contends that planning in France, by consultation and negotiation, does tend to drive the government into such close alliance with business interests that the planning board becomes a champion of firms it finds it easiest to deal with. Since these are usually the largest businesses, Sheahan points out, government planning thus has weakened competition.

A scheme of national economic planning here in the United States could well shift the focus of private enterprise even further away from dealing with market forces and meeting consumer demands, and toward reaching an accommodation with the ever more powerful government bureaucracy. The payoff under those new conditions for traditional consumer market research might be far less than from new efforts to persuade the government to adopt more generous production targets for the particular industry. I can readily conjure up visions of civilian companies following some of the practices of that branch of American industry which is now most closely tied to government decision-making. I mean the defense companies. Business financing of hunting lodges and fishing trips for civilian government planners might merely be a follow-up to the older defense industry tradition. But I suggest that such public sector marketing activities would be a low priority use of business resources. Yet given the incentive of any organization to try to survive and prosper in whatever environment it faces, I wouldn't be surprised if that type of marketing activity grew under a system of strong national economic planning.

Let me sum up very briefly. Even discounting the very serious shortcomings that exist in business planning, the differences between business and government decision-making are fundamental. Business planning is based on the traditional assumption that the ultimate decisions on the allocation of resources in society are to be made by individual consumers. An important corollary is that if a company guesses wrong about what consumers will buy, it will suffer the consequences. (As for government, incidentally, if you hear a lot about Lockheed bailouts and Penn Central bailouts and all that, remember, these are the most government-oriented, government-regulated, government-dependent parts of the supposed private sector. They are an indication of the shape of things that might come.) Government planning, implicitly or explicitly, is based on a fundamentally different set of assumptions from business planning. Government determines what it considers to be the society's overall interest, but if the public does not respond accordingly, it is not the planners who are presumed to be at fault. Rather, the public must be persuaded to accommodate to the

planner's view of the good or great society through
the development of new and more effective devices.
The greatest danger of centralized economic planning
is that it will, perhaps unintentionally at first but inevitably as its initial results prove disappointing, pro-
pel our society toward greater government controls
over individual behavior. We'll wind up incor-
porating into the planning structure, I'm afraid, not
just the Council of Economic Advisers and the
Federal Reserve System, but my goodness, perhaps
the FBI and the CIA.

  *Each panelist was given five minutes for rebut-
tal. Their remarks follow:*

JOHN KENNETH GALBRAITH: Well, I promise you I
won't require much time because our position has
emerged virtually intact. This does not in any way
denigrate the debating techniques that Murray
Weidenbaum has deployed here with his usual skill.
You will notice that he changed an argument for
planning into one, I quote, for "planning the whole
American system." This is a technique of translating
an argument of a moderate sort into a form which
could not be countered even if a man of Murray
Weidenbaum's skill were on the other side. It is a
technique that does not require any warning from
me.
  You will also notice how he managed to get on
both sides of the question. He warned against planning because it would be an excessive exercise of
power. And he also warned against it because it
would be ineffective against the great corporations.

That's another reason so skilled a debator cannot lose. My impression is that those are the two points on which Murray Weidenbaum rested his case.

I take issue with him on one other matter, which really has nothing much to do with this discussion. He points out that the development of socialism in our time is something which is no longer really advanced by the propaganda and beliefs of socialists, no longer spearheaded by URPE, but which is led by the great corporations. A marvelous thing and one has to admire the enormous flexibility of the modern corporate mind once it begins to lose money. The most ardent exponents of free enterprise immediately become proponents of socialism. And I would like to urge upon Murray as a friend that this is not peculiar to firms that are close to the government. One looks around at Chrysler and British Leyland in England, Alfa Romeo in Italy, the slightly ambiguous case of Volkswagen, Renault—practically the whole automobile industry is becoming a public utility. Even the big Wall Street firms sought a kind of guarantee for customers that was not thought wise for New York City bonds. I would like to suggest that whenever a firm is large enough, we'd better face the fact that it won't be allowed to fail. Socialism is preferred.

HENRY WALLICH: At this love feast, let me first make a comment on my own sinful past. Ken commented on the quality of the forecasts of the Council of Economic Advisers, to two of which I plead guilty. Ken is certainly right that we didn't hit the nail on the head. Maybe it would have been possible to do better. But I think I can say this: that through Republican and Democratic administrations, with one outstanding exception, the forecasts were pretty much in the mainstream of existing forecasts; and to say that they weren't very good, as Ken rightly does, is really to say that forecasting in general wasn't very good. One exception I have in mind is the forecast in 1971—*1066 and All That*—which was based I might say, on an advanced model and less on politics. So Ken is quite right, the forecasts haven't been very good. I don't know anybody who can do better, and if we need good forecasts for planning, then we'd better continue with our present unplanned processes.

Second, I do not think we need to get ideological about this and I hope we didn't. I do not identify planning with anything undemocratic. I think there are three major social dimensions: there's the market system versus planning, at one extreme or the other;there is private and public ownership; there is democracy and authoritarian government. These are all dimensions which I think are independent of each other. There is no reason, for instance, to associate planning with totalitarianism or with public ownership; all possible combinations of these three are at least conceivable and most of them have occured historically. What we're talking about here are matters we all know more or less as within the range of reasonable differences of opinion.

I would like to point out, however, that there are international differences, if I may revert to my earlier theme that planning may have worked elsewhere but probably would not do as well in the U.S. Murray referred to the intimacy of government and business in a country like France; he certainly could have added Japan, where planning is effective. Now you may think this is good or bad, but at any rate it does make for effective performance if there is a degree of intimacy of that kind. The U.S. Government does not generally have that kind of relationship with business. I think an excessive intimacy of regulators with the regulated industry is certainly bad. But when you have a predominantly critical attitude on the part of government—with respect to the regulated—that will not make for an efficient planning process. It is going to make for adversary proceedings, and, I suspect, for less effective planning performance. You see much of that kind of thing today when you think of the various measures imposed on business to further the very desirable causes of the environment, of the consumer, and so forth.

Finally, let me say something about the pending bill which surely is well-intentioned, and does not go very far—the Humphrey-Javits Bill. When you look at this, you see that cabinet members are going to sit on a council to be headed by the chairman of the planning board. I can just see the cabinet members coming en masse to sit under the chairmanship of a professor. The chairman would be lucky if he got the assistant secretaries to come. I think (a) that the bill is politically implausible, and (b) to the extent that it could be effective, the results would be a political compromise. The plan would be a document put together by the top politicians of the administration. It would not, I think, reflect technical expertise. It would predominantly reflect the way in which the

State Department, the Department of Agriculture, and the Department of the Interior, can best live with each other. All that does not lead me to think that this particular bill is even effectively designed to accomplish its own purposes. And, I revert to my original theme: it's just very difficult even to plan for planning in the United States.

MELVILLE J. ULMER: I thought that Kenneth Galbraith's defense of planning was so impregnable and overwhelming of the opposition that it leaves me with practically nothing to say. I'm just going to refer to one or two very little things because he didn't leave me anything else. First of all, the complaint of Mr. Weidenbaum is that business planning is so poor, helpless and ineffectual that how can we expect government to do any better? I really question whether business planning has been so bad. I was listening to Professor Melman earlier today, and he described in very well-documented detail how extremely effectively the military-industrial complex has managed to plan its affairs in its own interest. It has been so effective in absorbing much of our human as well as material capital of the very best quality, that it leaves the rest of the economy desperately in need of some new move to save itself. That new move is what I have been calling planning. Let's agree that there are business firms outside the military-industrial complex that have not done so well in their planning; that's true. But if you want to find out why (the Edsel has been worked to death, and how many years ago was that?), with very few exceptions it has been because the corporations have

not been able to control the general national level of
production and employment. And they do not
know—nor does any of us know—when a new recession may develop. By the decision of the present
government (and I don't mean the administration, I
mean the *kind* of government we have) recessions are
periodically generated. So are extreme inflations.
Now under these circumstances it is very difficult for
business firms to plan. The environment is volatile.
That problem would disappear, Mr. Weidenbaum
may be gratified to learn, under national planning.
Because the stability of the economic environment
would definitely, I think, be the first order of
business under planning. Stabilize at a full employment level, and stabilize the price level. I think these
things can be done and I think that business planning
under those circumstances would show spectacular
recovery.

I have only one other point and that has to do
with France. I do not think we ought to yield to the
temptation to equate words and deeds. We are told
time and again that there is planning in France. But it
really is very difficult, if you get away from their official literature, to find any evidence of that planning. It's true that they go through the motions
ritualistically, but there is actually very little planning
done so far as I can find out. They do have the for-
malities. I don't think they have the substance. And it
may be because big business in France wasn't about
to tolerate the kind of activity that real, legitimate
planning would involve. So if they don't have the
results, it's because they don't have the planning.

MURRAY WEIDENBAUM: I always learn a lot listening to the distinguished memebers of this panel. Today has been no exception. Unfortunately I don't have time to go into any details as to what those specific contributions to knowledge were, and you'll pardon me if I skip over that part. There are a few items I do want to take up. One is Professor Ulmer's—*in absentia* Professor Melman's—analysis of the power of business planning. As an erstwhile business planner, I recall, I hope accurately, a few lines from *Henry IV.* "Hang yourself brave Crillon. We fought at Arques but you were not there." I hasten to add the next line, "But we love you all the same."

Let me turn to another key point in the discussion. And that is the serious problems that face our society which have led to the cry for a formal national economic planning system. The problem that I read most about is the energy crisis or shortage. I think that's very instructive. Since the fall of 1973 we as a society have known about that problem, or catastrophe, or crisis. There hasn't been a shortage of planning since the fall of '73. There has simply been an inability to make difficult decisions. I see nothing in any of the formal planning systems that will change that.

One last little point; otherwise I wouldn't want to quarrel with my colleague and friend, Henry Wallich, who stated that in regard to our discussions on planning, we're only talking about more or less. I want to make it quite clear—I'm talking about less.

Reprinted by Permission of Challenge

APPENDIX II
BALANCED GROWTH AND
ECONOMIC PLANNING ACT
OF 1975

94th CONGRESS
1st SESSION

S. 1795

IN THE SENATE OF THE UNITED STATES

Mr. HUMPHREY (for himself and Mr. Javits) introduced the following bill;

A BILL

To amend the Employment Act of 1946 by providing for the development and adoption of a Balanced Economic Growth Plan, and for other purposes.

Be it enacted by the Senate and House of

*Representatives of the United States of America
in Congress assembled,*
That the Employment Act of 1946 is amended by
adding at the end thereof the following new title:
"TITLE II
BALANCED GROWTH AND ECONOMIC PLANNING
"SHORT TITLE
"Sec. 201. This title may be cited as the
'Balanced Growth and Economic Planning Act of
1975.'
"FINDINGS
 · "Sec. 202 (a) The United States is suffering its
worst economic decline since the 1930's. The combination of severe inflation and recession has
disrupted the nation's economy and has caused hard-
ship for millions of Americans. Recession and inflation have both revealed basic structural deficiencies
in the United States economy and have been intensified by conflicting and erratic short-term economic
policies without in many cases providing long-term
solutions.

"(b) The failure to develop a long-term national
economic policy has also created fundamental im-
balances in the economy.

"(c) No single Government agency is responsible
for acquiring a current detailed view of the national
economy and its component interrelationships and
the data necessary to maintain such a picture.
Without such information, it is not possible adequately to analyze the economy, to anticipate and
identify emerging problems, or to advise the President and the Congress about timely and effective ac-

tion. Government data collection must be better coordinated and systematized and information should be in a form that permits the identification in detailed comparison of major available options.

"(d) Although the Federal Government plays a major role in the nation's economy, the United States has no single governmental body engaged in the systematic and comprehensive formulation of national economic goals and policies. The formulation of long-term national economic goals, the identification of available and potential labor, capital, and natural resources, and recommendations for policies to reconcile goals and resources would enable the Federal Government to determine and rationalize its own impact on the national economy. These activities would provide assistance to State and local governments and the private sector by permitting action with greater knowledge of the nation's economic direction.

"(e) The establishment of an agency to recommend to the executive and legislative branches consistent long range economic goals and priorities, and policies to provide for their realization, would fill a major national need.

"(f) Individual economic security and personal well being are essential requirements to balanced growth in a free society. The economic decisions of the Federal government have direct impact on the lives of individual citizens. It is therefore necessary to provide a process of open and democratic planning for the future to enable the citizens of the United States to participate fully in the making of policies affecting the national economy.

"(g) The Congress finds that the formulation of national economic goals, consistent with the nation's economic resources and the identification of coherent policies to realize those goals are important national requirements which will achieve balanced economic growth and promote the economic well being of all of our citizens.

"PURPOSES

"Sec. 203. The Purposes of this title are to:

"(1) Establish an Economic Planning Board in the Executive Office of the President with responsibility for anticipating the Nation's economic needs, measuring available national economic resources, assuring an adequate supply of industrial raw materials and energy, outlining economic goals, and in the light of long-range economic trends and opportunities, for developing a proposed Balanced Economic Growth Plan, and recommending policies to achieve the objectives of the Plan.

"(2) Provide for the development of a Balanced Economic Growth Plan, embodying coherent and realizable long-term economic goals, consistent with the Nation's economic resources and identifying the policies and actions that would be required to attain such goals.

"(3) Provide for the continuing and systematic access by the Economic Planning Board to economic information and data required to prepare, review, and revise the Balanced Economic Growth Plan and to evaluate implementation of the Plan, and for the general dissemination of such information and data in accordance with this act to promote widespread, informed and effective public participation in the planning process.

"(4) Provide for appropriate participation by State and local governments and regional organizations, business, labor, consumers, other interested groups, organizations, and private citizens in the development and revision of such Plan.

"(5) Provide for Congressional review of each proposed Balanced Economic Growth Plan and for the approval or disapproval of the Plan by concurrent resolution of the Congress.

"(6) Establish procedures whereby the departments and agencies of the Federal Government will contribute to the continued assessment and implementation of the Balanced Economic Growth Plan.

"ECONOMIC PLANNING BOARD

"Sec. 204. (a) There is established in the Executive Office of the President an Economic Planning Board (referred to in this title as the 'Board'). The Board shall be composed of 3 members who shall be appointed by the President, by and with the advice and consent of the Senate. The Board shall be composed of persons of diverse backgrounds and experience. The President shall designate one of the members of the Board as Chairman.

"(b) The Board, shall—

"(1) prepare and submit to the Council on Economic Planning a proposed Balanced Economic Growth Plan, as provided in section 208 (a), for approval by the Council;

"(2) seek the active participation by regional,

State, and local agencies and instrumentalities and
the private sector through public hearings and other
appropriate means to insure that the views and proposals of all segments of the economy are taken into
account in the formulation of the Plan;

"(3) evaluate and measure the achievement of
the goals and objectives contained in any approved
Balanced Economic Growth Plan and report thereon,
as provided in section 208 (b);

"(4) review major programs and activities of the
Federal Government to determine the extent to which
such programs or activities are consistent with any
approved Plan;

"(5) coordinate the long-range planning activities of the departments and agencies of the
Federal Government to assume maximum consistency of such activities with the goals and objectives
stated in an approved Plan; and

"(6) carry out such other functions pertaining to
long-term economic planning as the President may
direct.

"(c) The Board is authorized—

"(1) to appoint and fix the compensation of,
such specialists and other experts as may be necessary
to carry out the functions of the Board, the Council
or any advisory committee under this title, without
regard to the provisions of title 5, United States
Code, governing appointments in the competitive
service, and without regard to the provisions of
chapter 51 and subchapter III of chapter 53 of such
title regarding classification and General Schedule
pay rates: and subject to all such provisions, to
appoint and fix the compensation of such other of-

ficers and employees as may be necessary for carrying out such functions;

"(2) to procure temporary and intermittent services to the same extent as is authorized by section
3109 of title 5, United States Code;

"(3) to contract with any public agency or in-
strumentality or with any person or organization for
the performance of services in furtherance of the
functions and responsibilities of the Office; and

"(4) hold such hearings at such times and places
as deems advisable, and administer oaths and af-
firmations to witnesses.

"(d) (1) Section 5313 of title 5, United States Code, is
amended by adding at the end thereof the following:

"'(13) Members of the Economic Planning
Board.

"DIVISION OF ECONOMIC INFORMATION

"Sec. 205. (a) There is established in the Board a
Division of Economic Information through which
the Board is authorized to secure information, data,
estimates, and statistics directly from various departments, agencies, and establishments of the Executive
branch of government. All such departments, agencies, and establishments shall furnish the Board any
available material which it determines to be necessary
in the performance of its duties and functions (other
than material the disclosure of which would be a
violation of law). The Board is also authorized upon
agreement with the head of any such department,
agency, or establishment, to utilize its services,
facilities, and personnel with or without reimbursement, and the head of each such department, agency,

or establishment is authorized to provide the Director such services, facilities, and personnel.

"(b) The Board shall carry out a program to insure the dissemination of economic data, statistics, and information in such form and manner as will provide a basis on which State and local governments, private enterprise, and the Federal government can make informed economic decisions and participate effectively in the planning process carried out under this title.

"(c) (1) The furnishing of any information, data, estimates, or statistics under this title by any person acting independently or pursuant to a requirement established under this title shall not be a violation of or evidence of a violation of any of the antitrust laws of the United States.

"(2) Disclosure of any information, data, estimates, or statistics in violation of any rule or regulation promulgated by the Board or the disclosure of any trade secret or proprietary information or any other information furnished to the Federal Government on a confidential basis by any person in the exercise of functions under this title shall be a violation of section 1905 of title 18, United States Code.

"COUNCIL ON ECONOMIC PLANNING

"Sec. 206 (a) There is established in the Economic Planning Board a Council on Economic Planning (referred to in this title as the 'Council') which shall consist of—

"(1) The Chairman of the Economic Planning Board, who shall be the Chairman of the Council;

"(2) the Secretary of State;

"(3) the Secretary of the Treasury;

"(4) the Secretary of Defense;

"(5) the Secretary of the Interior;

"(6) the Secretary of Housing and Urban Development;

"(7) the Attorney General;

"(8) the Secretary of Transportation;

"(9) the Secretary of Agriculture;

"(10) the Secretary of Commerce;

"(11) the Secretary of Labor;

"(12) the Secretary of Health, Education, and Welfare;

"(13) the Chairman of the Federal Reserve Board;

"(14) the Chairman of the Council of Economic Advisers;

"(15) the Director of the Office of Management and Budget;

"(16) the Administrator of the Federal Energy Administration; and

"(17) the Chairman of the Advisory Committee on Economic Planning.

"(b) It shall be the function of the Council to review and make such revisions as it deems appropriate in the Balanced Economic Growth Plan as submitted by the Board under section 204, and, upon approval of the Plan, to transmit the Plan to the President, and to review, on a regular basis, progress made in the implementation of the Plan. The Council shall adopt such rules for the conduct of its business as it may deem proper.

"ADVISORY COMMITTEE ON ECONOMIC PLANNING

"Sec. 207 (a) To furnish advice and assistance to the Board in the preparation and review of the Plan, there is established an Advisory Committee on Economic Planning which shall consist of—

"(1) four members appointed by the President;

"(2) four members appointed by the Speaker of the House of Representatives; and

"(3) four members appointed by the President of the Senate.

The Committee shall elect a Chairman, and shall meet at the call of the Chairman, but not less than twice a year. The members of the Advisory Committee shall be appointed from among representatives of business, labor, and the public at large, who are compentent by virtue of training or experience to furnish advice to the Board on the views and opinions of broad segments of the public in matters involved in the formulation and implementation of the Balanced Economic Growth Plan. Each member of the Advisory Committee shall be entitled to be compensated at a rate equal to the per diem equivalent of the rate for an individual occupying a position under level III of the Executive Schedule under section 5314 of title 5, United States Code, when engaged in the actual performance of his duties as such a member, and each member shall be entitled to reimbursement for travel, subsistence, and other necessary expenses incurred in the performance of his duties.

"(b) The Advisory Committee is authorized to establish regional or industry subcommittees to furnish advice and assistance to it in the formulation and implementation of the Plan. Any such subcommittee shall consist of at least one member of the Advisory Committee and shall be broadly representative of the particular region or industry, including business, labor, and consumer interests.

"THE BALANCED ECONOMIC GROWTH PLAN

"Sec. 208 (a) Not later than April 1, 1977, and biannually thereafter, the President shall transmit to the Congress a proposed long-term Balanced Economic Growth Plan prepared by the Director and approved by the Council. The Plan shall—

"(1) establish economic objectives for a period to be determined by the Board, paying particular attention to the attainment of the goals of full employment, price stability, balanced economic growth, an equitable distribution of income, the efficient utilization of both private and public resources, balanced regional and urban development, stable international relations, and meeting essential national needs in transportation, energy, agriculture, raw materials, housing, education, public services, and research and development;

"(2) identify the resources required for achieving the economic objectives of the Plan by forecasting the level of production and investment by major industrial, agricultural, and other sectors, the levels of State, local, and Federal Government economic activity, and relevant international economic activity, for the duration of the Plan; and

"(3) recommend legislation and administrative actions necessary or desirable to achieve the objectives of the Plan, including recommendations with respect to money supply growth, the Federal budget, credit needs, interest rates, taxes and subsidies, antitrust and merger policy, changes in industrial structure and regulation, international trade, and other policies and programs of economic significance.

"(b) The President shall submit to the Congress with the proposed Plan a Report prepared by the Board and approved by the Council. The report shall—

"(1) provide whatever data and analysis are necessary to support the objectives, resource needs, and policy recommendations contained in the Plan;

"(2) provide an examination of longer-term economic trends beyond the period of the Plan and recommend objectives with respect to the goals outlined in subsection (a) (1) :

"(3) compare the actual results with respect to matters referred to in subsection (a) since the submission of the previous Plan with the projected results of the Plan when submitted and indicate (A) the reason for any failure to achieve the objectives of that Plan, (B) the steps being taken to achieve the objectives of the previous Plan and (C) any necessary revisions in the Plan.

"STATE AND LOCAL PARTICIPATION

"Sec. 209 (a) The Board shall establish procedures to insure widespread consultation with regional, State, and local planning agencies in preparation of the Plan.

"(b) At the time of submission of any proposed Plan to the Congress, the President shall transmit copies of the Plan to the Governor of each State and to other appropriate State and local officials. Within

60 days from the submission by the President to Congress of the proposed Plan, the Governor of each State may submit to the Joint Economic Committee a report containing findings and recommendations with respect to the proposed Plan. Any such report submitted by a Governor shall include the views and comments of citizens within the State, after public hearings have been held within the State.

"(c) Upon the request of any regional, State or local planning agency, the Economic Planning Board shall review the plan of such agency to determine its consistency with the Plan and recommend changes to bring such plan more fully into conformity with the Plan. Funds available to such an agency under section 701 of the Housing Act of 1954 may, in accordance with such regulations as the President may prescribe, be used by such agency for the purpose of making such changes.

"CONGRESSIONAL REVIEW

"Sec. 210 (a) Each proposed Balanced Economic Growth Plan shall be referred to the Joint Economic Committee of the Congress. Within 60 days after receipt by the Congress of such proposed Plan, each standing committee of the House of Representatives and each standing committee of the Senate and each joint committee of the Congress shall submit to the Joint Economic Committee a report containing its views and recommendations with respect to all matters contained in the Plan which relate to matters within the jurisdiction of each such committee. The reports by the Committee on the Budget of the Senate and the Committee on the Budget of the House of Representatives shall contain the recommendations of such committees respecting budget policy for the duration of the Plan.

"(b) The Joint Economic Committee shall hold such hearings for the purpose of receiving testimony from Members of Congress, appropriate representatives of Federal departments and agencies, the general public, and interested groups as the committee deems advisable. The Committee shall also consider the comments and views on the proposed plan which are received from State and local officials under section 209.

"(c) Not later than 105 days after the submission of a proposed National Economic Plan to the Congress, the Joint Economic Committee shall report to the House of Representatives and to the Senate a concurrent resolution which shall state in substance that Congress approves or disapproves the proposed Plan, in whole or in part, and which may contain such alternatives to, modifications of, or additions to the Plan as the Committee deems appropriate. The report accompanying such concurrent resolution shall include findings and recommendations of the Committee with respect to each of the main recommendations contained in the proposed Plan. The Joint Economic Committee may from time to time make such other reports and recommendations to the House and Senate as it deems advisable.

"(e) Not later than 135 days after submission of a proposed National Economic Plan to the Congress, the Congress shall act upon a concurrent resolution reported under subsection (c). Upon adoption of any such resolution, a copy thereof, together with a copy of any report or document prepared by any committee of either House or by any joint committee in connection with the consideration by the Congress of the Proposed Plan shall be transmitted to the President.

"(e) There are hereby authorized to be appropriated to the Joint Economic Committee such sums as may be necessary to enable it to carry out its functions under this section.

"FINAL ADOPTION OF PLAN

"Sec. 211 (a) Upon receipt of a concurrent resolution pursuant to section 208, the President may make such modifications as he deems appropriate in any part of the Plan which was disapproved or which was not approved by the Congress, and shall publish a copy of the Plan, together with a copy of the concurrent resolution and all reports and documents accompanying such resolution, except that, if the concurrent resolution disapproved the entire proposed Plan, the President shall revise the Plan and resubmit it to the Congress not later than 30 days after the receipt of the concurrent resolution. Not later than 30 days after receipt of a revised Plan under the preceding sentence, the Congress shall, by concurrent resolution, approve or disapprove, in whole or in part, the revised Plan.

"(b) The President directly, or acting through the Board, may not take any action under section 212, and the Board may not take any action under such section, with respect to any part of the Plan which has not been approved or which has been disapproved by the Congress.

"EXECUTIVE BRANCH IMPLEMENTATION OF THE PLAN

"Sec. 212 (a) The President, with the assistance

of the Board, shall take appropriate actions to insure that the departments and agencies of the executive branch will carry out their programs and activities in such a manner as to further the objectives of the Plan, and to encourage State and local governments and the private sector to carry out their programs and activities in such a manner as to further the objectives of the Plan.

"(b) Whenever the Board determines that any department or agency of the Federal Government has submitted any budget request to the President or the Congress, or proposed any legislation, rule or regulation, or undertaken any other activity which may have a significant effect on the achievement of the goals and objectives contained in an approved Balanced Economic Growth Plan, the Board may require the head of such department or agency to submit a detailed statement to the Board assessing the consistency of the proposed budget, legislation, rule, regulation, or other action, with the Plan, together with the reasons for any significant departure from such goals and objectives.

"DIVISION OF BALANCED GROWTH
AND ECONOMIC PLANNING

"Sec. 213 (a) There is established within the Congressional Budget Office a Division of Balanced Growth and Economic Planning (hereinafter referred to as the 'Division') to perform long-term economic analysis. The Division shall be headed by a Deputy Director who shall perform his duties under the supervision of the Director of the Congressional Budget Office and shall perform such other duties as may be assigned to him by the Director. Such Deputy

Director shall be appointed in the same manner, serve for the same period, and receive the same compensation as the Deputy Director provided for in section 201 of the Congressional Budget Act of 1974.

"(b) It shall be the responsibility of the Division to assist the Joint Economic Committee in the discharge of its duties under this act and to provide—

"(1) information with respect to long-term economic trends, national goals, resource availability, and the economic policies necessary to achieve balanced long-term economic growth,

"(2) information necessary for the preparation of the report and concurrent resolution identified in section 210 (d), and

"(3) such related information as the Committee may request.

"(c) At the request of any other committee of the House of Representatives or the Senate, or any joint committee of Congress, the Division shall provide to such committee or joint committee the information necessary to fulfill their responsibilities under section 208 (a).

"AUTHORIZATION

"Sec. 214 There are authorized to be appropriated such sums as may be necessary to carry out the provisions of this title."

"RELATION TO THE COUNCIL OF ECONOMIC ADVISERS

Sec. 2. It shall be the duty of the Council of Economic Advisers to make an analysis of the relationship between the Economic Report and the Plan. The analysis of the Council shall be included in the Economic Report transmitted to Congress.

"ECONOMIC INFORMATION

Sec. 3. At the time of the presentation of the first Balanced Economic Growth Plan to Congress, the Division of Economic Information of the Economic Planning Board, at the direction of and with the approval of the Board, shall transmit to the Congress a report on economic data, statistics, and information, which shall contain the following:

(1) A review, carried out in conjunction with other departments and agencies of the Federal Government, of the activities, methods, and purposes of the infomation and statistical gathering, collation, analysis, and presentation functions of the Federal Government.

(2) An analysis of the existing information and statistical systems, and the economic data required under Section 204 of this act.

(3) Recommendations for the improvement or modification in the standards, methods, and systems of statistics and information gathering.

(4) Recommendations for such additional authority as may be necessary to obtain data not available under section 204 of this act.